Christine Thelker is 60 years old and has been living with Dementia since the age of 55. She lives in Vernon BC, Canada and spends her time advocating, writing and visiting with her family and friends. She especially enjoys her time with her little dog, Phoebe. Christine loves to walk, be close to the water and enjoys gardening. She is well-known for her positive attitude and her sense of humor. She loves to smile. Christine is proving that living well after a dementia diagnosis is possible.

Brenda

Remember Always

Be Brave
Be Grateful
Be Courageous

Stay Well

Christine Shelker
Aug 13/2020

I dedicate this book to all those who are fighting to live their best lives despite their diagnosis and to all those who work tirelessly to advocate and make the changes needed so that all living with dementia can do so with dignity and quality. I also dedicate these thoughts to my family at Dementia Alliance International for giving me the courage to speak out and to write. You have also provided me with a never-ending supply of hope and purpose...thank you.

Christine Thelker

FOR THIS I AM GRATEFUL

Living with Dementia

AUSTIN MACAULEY PUBLISHERS™

LONDON • CAMBRIDGE • NEW YORK • SHARJAH

Ordering Information:
Quantity sales: special discounts are available on quantity purchases by corporations, associations, and others. For details, contact the publisher at the address below.

Publisher's Cataloging-in-Publication data
Thelker, Christine
For This I am Grateful

ISBN 9781645756996 (Paperback)
ISBN 9781645756989 (Hardback)
ISBN 9781645757009 (ePub e-book)

Library of Congress Control Number: 2020907368

www.austinmacauley.com/us

First Published (2020)
Austin Macauley Publishers LLC
40 Wall Street, 28th Floor
New York, NY 10005
USA

mail-usa@austinmacauley.com
+1 (646) 5125767

One person, in particular, deserves special credit, my sister-in-law, Kay Przybille, who worked tirelessly to help me bring this book to fruition. Without her confidence in my dream and her dedication, this book would not be possible. I am deeply grateful and blessed by her presence in my life.

I would also like to acknowledge my doctors, Dr. C. Cunningham, and Dr. F. Pretorius, for their willingness to listen, to believe in me, and admit they may not have all the answers. Their readiness to learn and teach has helped me to live as fully as I can.

I could not have written this book without the love and support of my family and friends, for whom I am eternally grateful and thank all for their belief in me. Without you standing by, in the ready, through some very difficult times, I would not have persevered. This book is in honor of all of you. Special thanks to Shirley Burnham, Dallas Dixon and Kevin Bader who critiqued the book at various stages of production and gave me encouragement.

Lastly, to a few people whose lives mine would not have crossed if not for Dementia: Nichole Renee Kenney, for generously donating your time and talent for my cover photos, Fentisha Boswell, for all you do to advocate for me without expectation of any kind, and Julien Baylis for jumping in to be my BUB…without hesitation.

Foreword

In this book, you will not only learn from the personal experiences of being diagnosed with younger onset dementia, but also about living more positively with dementia. You will be jolted into one remarkable woman's reality of this disease. When I say reality, I do not only mean only the difficulties and significant challenges due to the acquired cognitive disabilities caused by any diagnosis of dementia, but equally, if not more so, the very great hurdles faced by all people with dementia on a daily basis due to the continued pervasive stigma, discrimination and 20th century attitudes towards people with dementia. You will also learn much about one Canadian woman who is both fearless, and resilient.

I've come to know Christine Thelker as a friend and fellow dementia advocate, since she became a member of Dementia Alliance International. Like me, she too has become an activist for people with dementia for human rights, and for the world to reframe dementia as a disability, as I have for the last decade, and as the World Health Organization and the United Nations have now for a number of years.

Also, like mine, and most others diagnosed with dementia, her experience after diagnosis was to be told there is nothing that can be done, and to get her end of life affairs in order, which I refer to as Prescribed Disengagement®. No rehabilitation. No disability assessment or proactive disability support. No support or advice to keep living positively. Frankly, this is not good enough, and until her last breath, I believe Christine will speak up for these things. Thankfully, this book will be one of her legacies when she can no longer speak.

She is a powerhouse, with much to say, and this book is the culmination of a lot of hard work, not only in terms of the time and dedication it takes anyone to write a book, but the work she has had to do, to support her cognitive abilities, to ensure she could still write, could still get her words out and down on paper. You see, some days, getting out of bed and getting dressed is like a marathon… we both live with mostly invisible disabilities, which means some days, functioning is a moment by moment thing.

Her book will expose you, in the true sense of that word, to the world of despair and sadness brought on by a diagnosis of dementia, but also to the joy and the humor. And I do mean joy and humor; for me personally, dementia is, in fact, the third greatest gift of my life, and being diagnosed aged 49, I feel I too have special insights, which have helped me to more intuitively, and more profoundly understand Christine's story.

If you choose to let it, having dementia will still mean having fun, although initially, many people will get lost in the sadness for some time as dementia is a terminal illness, and it does take a lot of courage to see hope again. The deep insights this disease can bring to some of us, the good, the bad and sometimes, the downright ugly, are openly unveiled as Christine tells her genuinely personal story.

One of the most difficult things many people with dementia will face is the 'dementia-doubters,' those individuals who don't believe we have dementia. As with many who have public profiles, Christine has had her fair share of them too, and for the record, it hurts to be doubted. The old adage, 'but you don't look like you have dementia,' or 'see, you remembered that, so you can't have dementia' are often the hardest to deal with, as we know our brains are failing, and we know what we can no longer do. But, if we focus on what we can't do, there is no hope for a future.

This wonderful book represents the reality of someone living with dementia, from the inside out, as Christine shares her insights with sincerity and candor as she takes you, the reader, on her journey. You will learn a lot about Christine, and even more on what it is like to live with dementia, and not only from the perspective of Pollyanna! It includes the stigma and discriminations she has faced, and that woefully, all people with dementia still face almost daily.

Perhaps the biggest challenge for those of us who are diagnosed still face, is not to be brought 'down' by those without a diagnosis, who often insist, it is all about us 'suffering' and of sadness. More likely, that is actually their experience, but it is not 'ours.'

Please do read Christine's wonderful book, not only with an open heart, but with an open mind, to the new possibilities of living with dementia. You will not be disappointed. I wasn't, and I hope it not only changes your world, but that it changes your thinking, and most importantly, your attitude to dementia.

Kate Swaffer
Author, Activist, Academic, Speaker
Australian Of the Year, South Australia, 2017

Global Leader, Women of Influence, Australia, 2018
CEO, Chair & Co-founder, Dementia Alliance International
www.kateswaffer.com

Book One
Patience

Chapter One

I want to go back a little bit, paint a picture, a picture of me, of my life, before the dementia, before the stroke, just before…

I was 55 years old working in a dementia unit and end-of-life care, two things that have always been near and dear to me. I took every opportunity I could to garner more knowledge, to be able to do a better job. I was a very big advocate…I always advocated for the patients, their families, the workers. I almost lost my job once, working tirelessly to have a couple obtain the right to die together in the same room. Taking care of, watching, working with the family taught all of us caregivers many things we still use today. Although I could have lost my job, I persevered because it was the right thing to do. That's just who I was.

I was widowed at 47 and have two beautiful stepchildren. Both Natasha and Brenden picked perfect partners to fit them in life's journey. They are such great young people. Natasha married first, in Penticton, on August 3rd, 2014. What a beautiful wedding! Jacob is a kind, caring, hardworking man; they make a lovely couple. On August 23rd, two weeks later, Brenden married in Calgary, on a golf course (perfectly fitting), to Erika. I will always be grateful that she came into his life. It was an emotional and proud time for me; I knew Uwe, my husband, was happy and smiling from the heavens. I missed him every day but I had rebuilt my life; it was now full and busy. My nursing jobs in Kelowna and Kamloops, plus my years in Vernon, had allowed me to make some very special friends.

Then there were my rocks, my husband's brother and sister-in-law, Brent and Kay. I remember Uwe telling me, the first time I was to meet them, that if something ever happened and I needed help, that's who I was supposed to call, that's where I was to go.

I love to travel, so I took trips to California, Mexico, Alaska, Hawaii, and many trips to the South Okanagan (especially Penticton), and to BC's coastal cities. I travelled on my own, with my sister and her husband, with numerous friends and other family members.

I travelled to Alberta to visit my kids: both were doing well with good jobs and building interesting lives with their spouses. I knew their dad was watching, feeling as proud of them both as I was. They would visit me here, I would go there, not as often as I would like but when I could.

I also held many dinner parties, BBQs, and get-togethers. I loved to plan and organize them, loved to prepare all the food, loved to see everyone relaxing and enjoying the visiting. I brought people together who may not otherwise have had the opportunity: people I worked with, friends and family. We always enjoyed our visits and it gave us all a chance to catch up; it always made me happy. I was a little social butterfly in that respect; very much my mother's daughter, always the road trip queen, be it for the day or the weekend or weeks on end.

Nothing made me smile more than getting in the car and heading off, my little dog, Phoebe, in tow. She is my best friend; she loves driving down the road with the top down, her ears flapping in the wind, always ready for the next road trip, a great travelling companion. I cannot imagine my life without her; she filled a void and took away many of the lonely hours. On the worst days, she would find a way to bring a smile to my face. I have many great memories of those trips.

I had, in 2013, bought my dream car, a custom design Mini Cooper S. Convertible. In 2014, I bought what I called my retirement home, my little yellow cottage, not big, just under 800 square feet, cute little front porch, large yard, big trees. I spent the next year having the inside painted. The kitchen was a pretty ocean blue, living room a soft butter yellow, bathroom a sea green. It was pretty inside and out, filled with things that brought me happiness: pictures of places where I travelled, pictures of good times with friends, it was a happy little spot. And I gardened, another passion. I loved to watch things grow. My spaghetti squash plants did so well, they were climbing the fence, the neighbor's tree, and out onto the road way. Everyone got squash. I took bags and bags to the Mission for the soup kitchen for the homeless.

I created a beautiful, quiet, peaceful sitting area. I planned to continue gardening so that by the time I retired, I would have created a space that was functional, pretty and easy to maintain. This was going to be my last little place. I could feasibly stay there forever, no stairs, easy access to town, my own little paradise. I enjoyed having company and entertaining, life was full, life was busy, I loved my job. I had rebuilt my life in a way that would allow me to look towards my retirement, and continue enjoying life. My work and home life felt balanced, all was good…

Chapter Two

Just before my first diagnosis (lacunar strokes and cerebrovascular disease), I started a blog called 'Through the Neuron Forest.' My writing was a way of helping the doctors and myself figure out what was happening to me. After that, it became about helping and sharing with others. I am hoping it will continue to help educate, inspire, give hope and purpose. If I help one person, I know having this disease had a purpose.

Friday, June 5, 2015

This blog is to try to help me remember things, document things, in part to help with my medical treatments and to help my family and friends as they try to support me.

Yesterday I needed medical attention but was unable to seek it out. I am not okay at these times; I cannot help me get what I need because my brain is on its own path while this is happening. Yesterday I remember thinking I don't feel right, then at some point the thing that kept going through my head was, just keep moving, just keep moving, so I did. I ended up walking into town, stumbling, coordination off, vision off, and my thoughts jumbled.

I thought I should sit down and call 911, but I didn't. My brain couldn't get the thought and action to go together. At one point I thought, *I'll just walk to the ambulance station; if I get there, they will know what to do.* Except that didn't happen either! Somehow, I ended up back home and then, what seems to me to be several hours, disappeared. In fact, it could have been much shorter. In any case, that time is gone, no recollection, not sure who I talked to or about what, remember thinking, *I should go to the hospital,* then thinking, *I will just rest, it will pass.*

Today I woke up and thought, *OMG, I should have gone to the hospital, this is not good!* I realized I needed somewhere to write what is happening, how I am feeling, and what's going on in my brain before – during, if I can – and after these episodes. Also, I feel many emotions, have many thoughts facing a journey such as this…so to find a place to put it…bring in my niece

Tara…thank you for setting this up, for being so willing to help me wade through the Neuron Forest.

Every day, if I feel good, I am doing what I can to enjoy this day, this hour, right now, and on days when I am not feeling right, I rest. Giving in to this has been a challenge; I am so used to multi-tasking, making decisions, taking care of others, it's hard to realize I am not able to do it all, that it's okay to just BE sometimes. I am always ready for the worst, hoping for the best, hoping to tackle my bucket list, wondering if the neurologists can actually do anything, or am I just slipping away little by little. I have a lot of hard decisions coming up and wonder how I will wade through them when my brain is not what it was.

Saturday, June 6, 2015

I am forgetful, not making sense today, jotting things as they come to me, a new reality for me. If I'm supposed to meet you for lunch, coffee, whatever, a reminder text from you is great…sometimes those memories are lost and I don't want to miss you. So please, a reminder helps me. I used to keep and juggle many things in my mind. Some days I still can but not all days. It's frustrating for me: a great organizer, great at multi-tasking. It's something I have always been proud of and yet, at only 56, to be losing all this is difficult. I get mad at myself; things that usually come to me quickly don't anymore. The best way I can describe the feeling is: picture the hourglass that spins on your computer while it's loading info. I feel I need one on my forehead to let people know to bear with me and wait; it's just taking a little longer than normal to load. Is everything going to come back to me in time? I hope so…

Some days it may seem I am not making sense, and it may in fact be true; it is part of the journey. If you are following this blog, I want you to understand that I am hoping this will be a reference for me to look back on, that will help me make decisions.

One hard thing is not being able to communicate with those around me during these bad events. I think I am making sense but I am not. The Heart and Stroke Foundation and many first responders claim that denial is one of the key indicators of a stroke among women. Women tend to be even more stubborn about getting help than men. Following is some of what Dr. Butler-Jones describes during his stroke, exactly how it is for me:

"I was trying to analyze what was happening to me," Butler-Jones from Halifax recalled. "I never considered it a stroke until the next morning when I was walking funny. Then I still tried to talk myself out of the fact that I was very weak on the left side."

Butler-Jones had what he calls 'left neglect' in which the brain doesn't pay attention to things on that side. "Often the stroke itself renders you incapable of identifying your problem and calling for help. You are paralyzed on one side, you can't get to a phone, you can't figure out how to dial a phone, and you can't make yourself understood. This was a real issue for me! My wife kept saying, "Shall I call an ambulance?" And I kept saying, "No, no, no, I just need to go to sleep," and that's not the thing to do. The next morning, when it was obvious I had had, fortunately, a small stroke she said, "So even though you're a doctor, I shouldn't listen to you, right? That's why it's important for all of us to recognize the signs of stroke.""

Sunday, June 7, 2015

On February 28, 2015, I was working evening shift, having a great shift, walked across the room, got a sharp pain in my head, sort of lost my balance for a minute, my vision was not right. I stopped; I remember thinking, *I must have moved too quickly*. Then I carried on to a patient's room. My working partner came to assist with the care; that is really the last I remember until I remember everyone staring at me. I kept trying to tell them I was okay. Later they said I was not making any sense. I was taken to emergency. From the accounts as told later by my nurse friend, Brenda, I had no concept of time, had difficulty answering questions, and looked vacant. I was hooked up, monitored, had an X-ray, ECT, and yes, I had suffered a TIA or mini-stroke. Within 48 hours, I was seen by a neurologist; the TIA clinic then waited for an MRI. The MRI has been done now; I have been fast tracked for the neurologist and more TIA help.

I have always dealt with reality head on. I normally make a decision and do it, whatever 'it' might be. Now I find myself procrastinating. Yikes, that's not who I am; it frustrates me, at times infuriates me. I just want to go back to how I was; I know this is not my normal behavior. Should I, shouldn't I, what is that all about? Well, okay, I guess it's part of my new reality. They say TIAs are a warning of what's coming; now I wait, but wait for what, the big one? Well, if that's what it's going to be, I pray it is really big! My worst fear, biggest fear, is this slow erosion. Somehow, I am hopeful that my doctors can do something. Will life be what it was? Not likely, but it can't stay in limbo either, can it? I am not good at limbo, I like to make decisions and just do it.

Sometimes I look in the mirror and wonder who I am now. It's important for my friends and family to know. Yes, I am strong, yes, I am positive, but I am also scared, sometimes a lot. I know everyone wonders if I should be alone. For me, that is my reality, I am alone. Do I give up my house? When and how will I make that decision? I still need to be me for as long as I can, I have to try to retrain my brain, I have a bucket list.

I realize to do a lot of things that I want to do I will have to do them alone. Everyone has jobs, husbands, children. I do not expect anyone to drop everything for me. Perhaps after more doctor appointments, I will be better able to make more decisions; for right now, it overwhelms me. Sometimes it makes me sad, sometimes it makes me crazy, but mostly it makes me try to enjoy each and every day to whatever degree I can. I am hopeful today.

Now I will wade through an enormous amount of terminology used by doctors about what's happening to me and I suppose once I see the neurologist, there will be a lot more. Is it a blessing or a curse that I work in health care; that I have a good understanding of what a lot of this means?

Lacunae Infraction

Many of the deep brain organs that can be injured by a lacunar stroke help to relay communication between the brainstem and the brain cortex or help to coordinate complicated body movements. In a lacunar stroke, brain cells in a relatively small area (measuring from 3 millimeters to as much as 2 centimeters across) are damaged or killed by lack of oxygen. Such a small area of brain destruction is called a lacuna. A lacunar stroke involves only a tiny area of the brain, but it can cause significant disability. The symptoms of lacunar stroke vary, depending on the part of the brain that is deprived of its blood supply.

Microvascular Ischemia

Microvascular ischemia is a condition where the small coronary arteries in the heart narrow, causing a reduction in blood and oxygen supply to a certain area of the heart. The condition can also affect the small vessels in the brain. Blood carries oxygen throughout the body, and ischemia can cause hypoxia (shortage of oxygen) to occur in the small arteries, which help to deliver blood from the heart to other organs in the body. This decrease in oxygen supply can cause severe damage to the heart and other organs, and the lack of oxygen can cause tissue to die. It can cause the heart to feel like it is cramping or being squeezed, creating a tightness in the chest. The person may feel nauseous or lightheaded because the brain or heart is not receiving enough oxygen. Pain in the shoulder or arm is also a common symptom of ischemia. Some people who have periodic ischemic attacks feel numbness, vertigo, or have trouble concentrating. More severe symptoms will occur if an artery becomes blocked.

Cerebrovascular Disease

The most common forms are cerebral and include the progressive deterioration of motor and sensory function. Hemorrhagic stroke occurs when a blood vessel in part of the brain breaks…

Coronary Cerebral Vascular Disease

The symptoms depend on the location and impact on brain tissue. I have a rare form of angina that attacks when resting or sleeping. I also have difficulty speaking, face paralysis, vision problems, loss of balance and loss of coordination at times. Inflammation in the arteries of my brain obstruct blood flow causing muscle weakness. Having Cardiovascular Disease (which affects the heart blood vessels) and Cerebrovascular Disease (which affects the brain blood vessels) at the same time increases the risk factors because one can impact the other, hence the name.

Monday, June 8, 2015

Back from my morning walk with my dog. What a beautiful morning! I have to be done walking by 7:15 or it gets too hot for Phoebe; I don't want her little feet to burn. I feel teary today, I don't like feeling this way, but guess I need to give into it now and then. Apparently, I am not Superwoman, and let me tell you that was hard to swallow! Just feeling overwhelmed, I guess; wishing I could start putting my life together in whatever way it needs to be. Waiting for answers is harder than getting them. It feels like everything I have worked so hard for is slipping away and yet I still have so much to be thankful for…emotions: they sure do crazy things to me. I'm trying to hold off making decisions right now; that's part of the emotional turmoil. I like to figure out what I need to do and then set out to make it happen, but in this case, I have no idea what needs to happen. Maybe I do and I'm just having trouble settling with it.

Add to that: this is generally an emotional week for me. Yesterday was my wedding anniversary, tomorrow will mark the eighth anniversary of Mom's passing, Friday will be 10 years since I lost Uwe (my husband). I don't know how I actually got here! There isn't a day in all those years that I haven't thought about them and missed them. Still, it makes me smile thinking about them. That's it, time to get busy, let the tears flow as they need to, perhaps a day of cleansing so to speak, and to breathe, really breathe.

Today I went on a day retreat for meditation and deep breathing. I realized as we were being taught how to do deep breathing exercises, that it is very likely I have not been breathing properly for years. So, I am going to continue working on deep breathing and relaxation meditation as part of my campaign to help myself. I realize I have basically been holding my breath, keeping myself reined in, in case something else happened…well guess what, it happened anyway! The other shoe dropped with this health crisis, so no matter what, laugh, breathe, enjoy…

I do know that my emotions are much more acute since my brain event, my sleep is messed up more than ever, adding to my apnea. It is so trying to fight through all these changes and leaves me exhausted. I seem to manage a day or two as long as I don't overdo it and then need a down day as the fatigue is unbelievable. That in itself is hard for me to accept, I, who am usually so full of energy, feel like I am moving at a snail's pace. Great, it's a frustration for sure, something else to adapt to! I have never struggled with change, always felt change was good and necessary, yet these changes in my abilities I now struggle with. But a long soak in a tub with Epsom salts and baking soda and nice cool water…an hour later with the meditating and deep breathing, I feel better. Calmer, the peacefulness has returned.

Wow, can't believe this day! My employer (Interior Health BC) mucked everything up for me, so I have no income at this time! They just give you one last kick. Now they want $400.00 a month for my benefits. My Employment Insurance still has not kicked in because of their mistakes; this makes a real hardship for me. I will be left with no choice but to sell my house, which I have been trying to prepare myself for, but would like to have been able to decide when. I will not make the definite decision until after the 20th, today I will just cry and cry some more.

My Record of Employment was done wrong multiple times causing the delays; then the $400.00 plus monthly for benefits came into play. (Those benefits are desperately needed.) I felt they should have delayed asking for monies until they corrected the errors that caused all the delays in my having monies coming in.

I believe I was originally diagnosed with apnea in about 2000 by the specialist in Kamloops, Dr. Navatril. Uwe first discovered the problem and used to shake me until I started breathing again. They never treated it until about 2007 when Dr. Cunningham sent me to the sleep clinic where I did two overnight tests.

Tuesday, June 9, 2015

Okay, my rant is over. I am still standing, just needed a meltdown, I guess. It is a beautiful evening, tomorrow will dawn a new day, and things will unfold as they are meant to.

After yesterday's emotional day, it feels good to wake up feeling less stressed, knowing through the power of prayer and my faith, that I will be okay. I am really trying to pay attention to the emotional side of this journey as I know it is one of the things for sure affected.

My face is partially numb again; this happens a lot. I am actually getting used to it. I sleep in blocks of time: 45 minutes to an hour, then I am up. My best hours of the day are between 5 AM and 2 PM; after that, fatigue becomes a real factor. I am hoping for a good day today, without sharp pains in my head, just a relaxing day making the best of what I have. I am hoping that by the end of June, I will be well on my way to having all the big decisions made, getting rid of as much as possible that causes any stress. It is days like yesterday that you really miss your partner, someone to share the load, someone coming home at the end of the day, someone to share the beauty of the morning. It's at those times the actuality of how alone I am, resonates within me. I know I am not entirely alone; I know I have great family and friends. I couldn't make it through this without them, they are what holds me together, they are my glue, and yet I am also aware that I am on my own. I am as okay as I can be and that's good enough.

Wednesday, June 10, 2015

Tonight, I feel calm and peaceful, thankful for the love of family and friends, knowing they love me through the bad days, and knowing that the bad days are a necessary part of this process. They won't all be bad. I am trying to still move forward in whatever fashion is possible. For tonight, as I sit on my front porch enjoying a quiet evening and thinking of the many things I am grateful for, I know that the decision (to sell my house) made today will also bring with it new challenges. I also know there will be much less stress because of it, so for today and every day while it is still mine, I will enjoy my pretty little front porch.

I am fighting the fatigue; I wake up as tired as when I go to bed. Yet I still make myself keep moving, I am still grateful to be up watching every sunrise, and still going for a walk with Phoebe. Somehow, I smile to myself and marvel at this journey. Every time a sharp pain courses through my head, I stop and wonder, is this a sign another TIA is coming? Then I analyze what has been happening up to this point trying hard to follow the erratic workings of my brain. I realize that the times I feel like someone is squeezing my chest like a heart attack, this too is part of the event. Is the brain talking to the heart or the heart talking to the brain? Will I ever know? I have always been fascinated with learning so I guess it makes sense that I would be trying to learn about this journey, and the biggest part of learning is by listening to my own body.

After much turmoil trying to work through the various processes needed because I am off sick, I actually met with my manager and spoke to her about arranging things better at Interior Health. None of us should have to fight; we should be able to focus on our recovery, not try to untangle a mess that we did not create. I believe we are fortunate to have her in place; she is someone who has heart. I believe she will follow up; I believe she was sincere in her apology for what I have had to wade through. I am just hoping changes will make it better for others who follow me. I am grateful for the support of those I work with.

Chapter Three

Thursday, June 11, 2015

Four very special ladies are taking me to lunch; I am so blessed with the support I have around me. Looking forward to much needed laughter because it is true, laughter is the best medicine. Had lunch the other day with Brent, the most amazing brother-in-law a girl could ever have. He helped me to make some decisions that have been weighing heavy. I have immense respect for both him and my oh-so-lovely sister-in-law, Kay; they have been my port in the storms of life for ten years now. I can't imagine how much more difficult a lot of those times would have been without them. There are so many great people in my circle. I know this is difficult for all those standing back watching, unable to do anything, and yet they all do so much just being there.

I struggle with the emotional roller coaster this has thrust upon me; even if I am sitting having happy thoughts, there are tears. I don't feel depressed, sad, or angry, just teary. It's like I am not in control anymore, my brain is, and it's not doing its job properly. I keep trying to retrain it; maybe it's going to retrain me.

I know Dr. Cunningham will help me do what is best for me. I hear so many people talk about how they don't like their doctors or that they don't feel their doctors actually hear them. This makes me very grateful for mine.

Friday, June 12, 2015

Approximately a week ago, I woke up about 2:30 AM. My chest felt like it was being squeezed so hard, pain going down my arms and up and across my jaw, but I know what to do. I take my two chewable aspirins that are always on my night stand, I drink a glass of water, also always beside my bed, I take my nitro spray, and I wait to see if it will settle down. I lay and focus on just breathing and eventually I am able to sleep.

The next day my left lower leg swells and I get checked at the walk-in clinic. Two days ago, another squeezing pain in chest, end up with pain in my head, vision blurry, coordination off. I sleep, I rest, then yesterday afternoon, after a lovely lunch with friends, my right leg and foot swells, I take pictures because it is so obvious, and may be more information for the doctor. Ross and Brenda (a nurse friend and used-to-be neighbor) bring me dinner; Ross cuts my lawn, I am grateful. I keep my legs up, double up on hydrochlorothiazide; this is only a short-term solution so what is the bigger question? Why? A lovely walk in the rain this morning, leg swelling is gone, feeling a little more rested.

When I got sick, I was hoping that in a short time I would be well enough to return to work. However, things deteriorated, my medical costs were soaring, I had no income, some days I could barely make it across the room, most days I was not really functioning but I kept trying to keep things done. I had a very large yard, I was trying to make it more low maintenance, but the work was too much, the money to do it was going towards health costs, I was watching all my hard-earned savings disappear. I sat with my banker and talked about the long-range forecast which was not good. He said looking after my health had to be my top priority.

My neurologists and my family doctor were telling me that sometimes it takes years to get a proper diagnosis and I continued to have TIAs. But things were not getting done. I knew it was nice of people to say, "Just let us know and we'll help," but those people had their own stuff to do and it was not realistic to think they could take care of my stuff too. I needed to sell, to downsize, to stop pushing my already sick body.

Saturday, June 13, 2015

Today has been good, slow, steady progress. I'm thankful to have my friend Terri (an old friend from Valemount where Uwe and I lived before he died) here, her support is unending. Yesterday was another emotional day. The decision is that the house will be listed Monday or Tuesday. Again, I am blessed to have such a good friend in my realtor, Rick, who is as always going above and beyond the call of duty to help me. I am so very blessed in so many ways. Terri and I have been packing up enough to de-clutter the rooms. My face is numb again. I am wondering now if it really will totally un-numb, or if the sensation is just gone.

Time will tell…

Sunday, June 14, 2015

I feel like running outside and yelling I am so happy. Today is the best day (so far anyways) that I have had in a long, long time. I am sitting relaxing. I plan on just enjoying each and every moment of it. I'm trying so hard to not over-do it, but even the fatigue seems to have lifted ever so slightly. So I will relax, smile a lot, be thankful for the kind words, and support from friends and family…just so truly thankful, grateful for this very good day.

Monday, June 15, 2015

I had such a good day yesterday until about 9:30 last night. I was sitting quietly relaxing, then a sharp pain in my head, blurry vision, another event…crap…and I am left with the after effects, brain fog, headache, unable to do some things. On we go.

It's been difficult trying to do the most basic things. I went to the lab for blood work, the nurse got it started, it stopped, veins collapsed she said, try again, in different arm, use all the tricks to try to squeeze a couple of small vials of blood. I go for an electrocardiogram tomorrow morning; too exhausted to attempt anything else today.

Tuesday, June 16, 2015

Five AM and I am up enjoying the lovely morning after a horrible day yesterday. By early evening, I was so frustrated with my condition. This morning brain fog has lifted, no after-effect headache, so hoping for a good day. I will keep smiling; I am still so very blessed and grateful.

Wednesday, June 17, 2015

Out to do a couple of errands and everywhere I went, someone would stop me and ask me if I was okay. My friend I was shopping with also thought I did not seem well. At times I felt like I'm just going to collapse, my body was so tired. I am hoping in six months I will be looking back going, *wow, that was an unbelievable journey.* And, mostly, I wish that this fatigue will be long over and I get back to somewhere close to where I was before. I'm still grateful for the day.

Thursday, June 18, 2015

(Step 1) My friend Terri left this morning. She spent the week getting so much done for me. I will be ever grateful. I woke up this morning feeling like I have taken three steps back. Terri said, while she was here, numerous times I was sitting or standing but that I appeared vacant, and that I had no color and looked like I was going to collapse, which was exactly how I was feeling but unable to verbalize it in a way that would make sense. I am grateful she was here and that this morning she was able to sum it up for me. I think, shouldn't I be getting stronger not weaker? Fight mode is to keep moving, you have to keep moving. My walks have decreased in distance a lot of days; I head out planning to do my four to five kilometers but can't get through much more than one or two. I will keep pushing.

Friday, June 19, 2015

(Step two) Off to the neurologist, grateful at how soon he got me in, expecting more tests to be ordered, not thinking he will have all the answers for me today but will be grateful I am moving in the right direction.

Saturday, June 20, 2015

(1 step back) Okay, I am a little overwhelmed at the moment. They cannot fix this; they can just try to minimize or deaden the circuits in my brain so that I don't feel them and perhaps in time function better than I am now. My neurologist said it is going to be a long process, these are extremely potent drugs which can also cause problems, so the dose will change every two weeks for eight weeks, I will go see him again in October. During that time, the dose may have to be changed, it can also make some of the symptoms worse, like speech, coordination, ability to process information, dizziness. All those things will be monitored closely. If these drugs don't work, we go back to the drawing board.

I don't need any more scans or Magnetic Resonance Imaging done, they know what's happening; those tests will not help. Trying to minimize the effects these events have are all they can do. So, we will play 'roll the dice' for a while. I am hoping it at least dulls things enough that my body has a chance to refuel. I will be happy with that. I will be laying low for a couple days till I see how these first doses affect me and check in with Dr. Cunningham by week's end. It is all very complex.

Sunday, June 21, 2015

I took my first dose last night. I think it will take a few doses to feel any impact. I am trying to figure out how I feel this morning. I think I will feel more confident once I have a chance to sit with my doctor and ask questions: a lot of questions. Like, if this is treating the symptoms, will it actually help with the fatigue that is on-going? How long can we expect the medication to work? If the medicine masks the TIAs, how will we know when I have one…will there be less or more?

I suppose the last question doesn't really matter if I am able to resume functioning with some kind of capacity more than I have been in the last number of months. I know I will have many more questions to add to the list, so I will observe myself while trying to get some rest. The neurologist wants me to keep notes, so the blog is perfect. I will be grateful for what I do have.

Monday, June 22, 2015

Today I am dizzy, my coordination is really bad, my head hurts, I feel nauseous, and I have so many questions for my doctor. Is this the right treatment plan or is it just a masking plan? Some things just don't seem to add up. Tomorrow I have to be up and about no matter what. I have to start fighting my way through again. I will find a way to get back to a version of myself that was there a few months ago. If I fight hard enough, I will overcome this too! Yes, many questions need answers. Again, I am feeling so grateful to have a doctor that I have confidence in.

My head hurts so bad I want to scream, but Dr. Meckling (my specialist) said there is no point going to the hospital anymore. I will see if Dr. Cunningham agrees. I am so nauseous I want to throw up, no appetite. I have to try to force some food in…and maybe, just maybe I will scream…fighting hard today.

I get these pains in my head when I have an event and if the event is a bad one, I later am left with what I call the hangover effect. But the pain in my head on these medicines is excruciating. This feels worse than the events did. Okay, time for the self-talk, it could be so much worse, so push through it, get moving.

The medication is meant to control the brain events, it will not stop them altogether, and the drugs will have to build up over time. More questions…what are the long-term effects of all the side effects??? My doctor appointment next week will hopefully bring about some answers. I now do 'juicing' (fresh fruit and whole vegetable smoothie) and have not in the last few days, been so sick from the medicines. This neurological disorder is an electrical issue in the brain; I'm short circuiting. Today I have fumbled my way through better than the last two days. Hoping, as the meds kick in, I will undergo some return to a re-energized me.

Tuesday, June 23, 2015

Noon. Just woke up for the third or fourth time today. Pins and needles, tingling, yuk, feel in such a fog. This is day five and was expecting more, expecting better. I had to force down a small amount of food, feel very off balance today, had high hopes this morning…just so, so tired. I am grateful that today I was able to take Phoebe for a walk in the lovely summer rain.

Wednesday, June 24, 2015

Although I am still not feeling great, I am better than yesterday. After a lengthy discussion with the pharmacist, he said, "Stop taking the meds, your system isn't tolerating them!" It will take a few days to get them out of my system. I left a message for Dr. Meckling. I have an appointment with my neurologist, Dr. Iqbal, in Abbotsford. He will take over my care July 22. I feel good about that. I know he will work to have me function to the best possible level without masking and overloading the body with drugs. I am determined to stay upright today, to get out with the living with a smile no matter the pain. I am strong.

Thursday, June 25, 2015

Had I not been able to understand that what was happening the last five days was not normal, I quite likely could have carried on taking the meds thinking, *oh well, they said I need it.* I could see the scared and worried looks on the faces of friends and family who stopped by to check on me. Their concern was warranted and noticed. I'm only awake for short bursts of time. Surely my angels have been whispering to me through this whole week to keep fighting. Yesterday, three good things happened for me: I got off the meds, got an appointment booked with my old neurologist, and got an offer on my house. So, in the midst of the bad, good things still happen. I hope tomorrow I will be able to walk without stumbling and stay awake for a few hours. Tomorrow I will enjoy the day no matter what because that's what I do.

I can feel the effects of the meds lifting; my vision is clear again. I was able to go for a nice walk without falling or stumbling, my coordination is returning…I am so very grateful. This could have had deadly results. In another day or two all the effects will be totally gone, I hope. It feels good to see and feel a small glimmer of myself again.

Friday, June 26, 2015

This morning I woke up feeling a little more like myself; I looked in the mirror and could actually see me looking back. I am still weak and tired but so much better than the previous week or so, another hurdle overcome, coming out the other side. I am hoping in the next couple days I can start to regain some of my strength. I'm taking it easy, taking it slow, and will be extra careful in this heat. I don't want any more setbacks.

Saturday, June 27, 2015

I will try to get out and about for a bit. I am thankful for so many great people who were checking on me. I will happily learn to live with these brain events rather than be drugged and end up like a zombie. I'm wondering if I can retrain my brain and slow the events down. I find the brain fascinating, even mine, even with its short circuiting. Today I feel as if my laughter and quirkiness is returning…yay!

Sunday, June 28, 2015

This morning in the very early hours, I realized that my brain never gets to rest. It is so active at night I wake up with thoughts and ideas going through my head which carry on into my day. It's deep thinking time when it should be deep sleeping time. I find it interesting.

I know I am not well enough to be at work at this point; I love my work but my body is just too tired right now. I believe that every time my blood pressure spikes, I have one of these brain events…I am analyzing, reviewing, trying to help myself. So, I am trying to create an environment with little stress (we all know stress increases blood pressure) that allows me to rest if I need to and do only as much as I feel I am up to. I will take away the excess responsibilities, sell the house, downsize to a place where all my energy is not used up trying to keep up with everything. Instead of pushing myself every day, I will be able to pace myself, enjoy more. Will these brain events ever stop? Not likely, but maybe I can manage them. I struggle right now trying to figure out what is next for me. I really just want to BE for a while; I can't really even explain it. Last night, on one of my many awake times, I was standing in the kitchen having a glass of water. The only thing that was in my mind so very clear was the phrase, 'Free Falling.'

Saturday, July 4, 2015

I have learned for the most part to manage my days, reschedule things as required, give my body the time to recover between events. So today I am grateful for all those who are helping me, and for waking up being able to make my own coffee and get myself outside to enjoy another day dawning.

Tuesday, July 7, 2015

So many thoughts, so many questions, so few answers. I am learning to let things unfold. I, for the first time, feel like I'm walking in quick sand, nothing solid under me, no ability to chart a path. So, I just let go, take whichever path is before me, just float along, drifting aimlessly. We are told we should have goals, one, three, five, ten-year goals. Well, not this time. I've been trying to force some decisions; I realize I need those decisions to come on their own. I want a holiday from all of this.

Thursday, July 9, 2015

For the last week or so, nose bleeds, which I have never had before, are a daily occurrence. My blood pressure is running low; not normal for me. When I'm lying down, my head stops hurting; as soon as I get up my nose bleeds and my head starts hurting. If I move around too much, my nose starts bleeding. I saw Dr. Cunningham yesterday and will see him again Monday. I so want to be able to function better than I am. I look awful, I know I do; I feel like I am just going to collapse. Hoping desperately that this is not my new norm. I am staying with friends for a few days. Hopefully, I will get feeling a little stronger soon.

Sunday, July 12, 2015

I have endured. I have always had a plan A and usually a plan B, always been able to adapt, change on short notice. No plan now; it is overwhelming me. Yesterday, I spend the day very quietly researching different things, letting ideas swirl around. This morning I woke up with some answers so made some decisions.

Wednesday, July 15, 2015

I have not been well; in my opinion I took a real slide backwards. I saw Dr. Cunningham on Monday and he wants another oximeter test (measuring oxygen in blood and heart rate) done. Is this more issues with my apnea?

Today I removed the computer chip out of my breathing machine and took it in to Al. He pulled up the results. Everything was great on the report until June 21; since then, it has been off the rails. That is the day after I started the trial medications. The big question is why? What happened? Did the medicine cause an event, did an event cause the change?

Thursday, July 16, 2015

This afternoon I went to pick up the oximeter and my breathing equipment. There is absolutely no problem with my equipment. So now the question is: as the medicines I was given are known to make the symptoms worse, did they do lasting damage? I feel like Sherlock Holmes trying to solve a mystery, except it's MY life that's being affected. I must be diligent, stay strong, and keep asking questions. Eventually, I will have solved the mystery of 'Chrissy's brain.' I must advocate for myself.

Friday, July 24, 2015

On my return from the coast, after conferring with Dr. Iqbal, I feel like we are making slow progress. I am on another trial with two new medications. I have been told again this condition cannot be cured. This is a neurological disorder that we can try to manage; this is something I have to live with and try to get to a point where I can have some stretches of being symptom free. Let's hope this trial helps.

Saturday, July 25, 2015

My walk was short, not because of me but because my dog does not like the rain. I did manage to do a fair bit, cleaned my bathroom, made some muffins, but now I have to rest because I am so nauseated. Okay, maybe I need more time. I expect too much of myself: still hopeful.

Friday, July 31, 2015

The second day of clear vision with no electrical currents pulsing through my head! Yesterday, I had enough energy to get a haircut, spend a few hours with my kids, and have a good day. I still do not feel quite myself but definitely better than the last couple of months. My eyes look clearer, I feel like I can go for my walk this morning and really enjoy it; hopefully, it will last the whole day. I am still at my best early then start to slide as the day progresses. Day two on a higher dose of the new medicines, so am hopeful things will get better and better.

Monday, August 3, 2015

Last night at around 1:30 AM, I decided to get something to drink; my coordination was off and I broke a glass. I cleaned up the mess and went back to bed. Up at 5 AM, feeling like I hadn't slept all night, brain fog, everything was off. Around 10:30 AM, I got a sharp pain in my head followed by blurry vision and bleeding nose. So, three decent days while on the second dose of new medication. Third dose starts tomorrow night, frustrated at best, feel like sitting down and crying, but going for a nap instead.

My friend Terri came and spent another week helping me pack, downsize, and organize. She was a true blessing at that time, I could not have managed without her, I was barely functioning. She also created a book with names, addresses and pass codes that I would need. There was so much she did and never complained. I am sure at times it must have been difficult for her to understand what was happening to me as I could not explain. I am truly grateful. Rick (my realtor) and his lovely wife, Jenny, dropped everything, came over and took care of all the details of selling my home. I don't remember a great deal of that time; I only know they were there taking care of things. My niece, Tara, held a garage sale of all the stuff Terri and I decided I would let go. She organized it and held it twice. I have very little remembrance of how that came to be; all I know is she was there, helping, supporting along with my other friends. They are all blessings.

Wednesday, September 2, 2015

Started another trial of new meds last night. I feel like me today, the me who I was wondering if I would ever see again. I'm hoping this time it will last and maybe, just maybe, we will have something that will work for more than a few weeks. I am still surprised at how much this has taken out of me, but I hope that once these neurological events are controlled (if that's possible), then perhaps I will have a better chance of fighting the fatigue.

Sunday, September 6, 2015

This is day five on new meds which have been adjusted twice. Overall, I have not felt this well in many months. I am keeping my fingers crossed these good days become great months.

In the beginning of September, 2015, I walked out of my little yellow house for the last time. I was noticing more and more that I was forgetting, getting confused. It became really important to me that my best friend and I have a road trip as I was feeling so uncertain about my future and still struggling to get a diagnosis. Barb (another nurse friend) and I decided we were going to the Oregon Coast: somewhere we had always talked about going. Everyone questioned her as to whether she was wise to be traveling with me given my state of health. What if I collapsed, what if I died...was I safe to be driving…and bless her heart, she said, "What if? I'm not worried, she wants to go and I'm going with her." Her husband, Ivor, said go…so off we went in my little mini convertible…top down…two best friends on an adventure.

By the time I left on the trip, I was settled into my girlfriend Sharon's house on East Hill. She had graciously offered me a place to stay for six months to allow me time to find accommodations and just breathe. What a gift that was! It was nice to have a place to be able to rest, to not worry. During that time, I underwent a big surgery to have all my teeth removed because (I was told) they interfered with my trigeminal nerve, a nerve that covers your brain and runs down the side of your jaw. It was a horrible surgery but I had it because I would do anything if it would help me get better. I was so hopeful that would fix all my troubles, but it didn't help at all.

In summary: The first neurologist I saw was Dr. Lai at the Kelowna Hospital Heart and Stroke department. He ordered new tests, MRIs, and set me up to work with the stroke clinic. From there, I was referred to Dr. Meckling because he had seen me in the past for a bad concussion.

Two years prior, I saw Dr. Iqbal, a neurologist in Kamloops, who was the MS specialist for the interior of BC, because at one point my doctor believed I had MS. By the time I returned to work in Vernon, I was healthy and fit with no medical difficulties. I was on my Norvasc and Hydrochlorothiazide to keep my blood pressure stable but otherwise healthy. He too saw me for this new problem.

Dr. Meckling was not in agreement with the latest report from my MRI which stated I had had a lacunar stroke. He felt maybe it was some type of seizure so sent me down the road of many different drug trials. Medications he tripled me on were: Levetiracetam, Sumatriptan, Ratio-Lenoltec, Lamotrigin, Gabapentin, Fosamax, and Accel-Topiramate.

When he told me he wasn't sure what was wrong, that he had lots of medications we could keep trying until we found something that worked, I was angry. It was like he wasn't listening. He couldn't tell me that I didn't have a stroke but felt I was too young, couldn't explain the spots on my brain or the area damaged, yet all my symptoms fit with a stroke. Then came the appointment that needed to happen, the appointment where he apologized to me, saying he was stuck; he couldn't seem to see the whole picture, said it happens sometimes, said we needed fresh eyes. I was then sent to Dr. Pretorious who reviewed all the tests and started tests of his own. Dr. Meckling's willingness to ask for someone else to help was in fact a gift; it was the first step in my eventual diagnosis.

Chapter Four

Wednesday, December 2, 2015

For the last week and a half, many lightning bolts have shot through my head making me tired, unable to focus, left side of face numb, doesn't feel right. Today, Ross looked at me and said, "Oh, you don't look good, the left side of your face is drooping and you don't look right." Four hours later, he said, "You look better now." I was feeling better but my face was still numb.

Tuesday, April 2nd, 2016

This is something one of my friends wrote about what was happening:

"Christine says her head hurts, she is stumbling, coordination is off, has difficulty expressing herself, looks extremely exhausted, is being very forgetful and confused. She seems to have had a lot of difficulty this week but continues to try which appears to leave her more exhausted, confused, and forgetful. She has difficulty describing what is happening, but she says her head does not feel right, lightning bolts, her vision is blurry, she feels unsteady and dizzy."

*****

At the beginning of April 2016, I moved from Sharon's into an old heritage house with a former working colleague. It had a beautiful wrap-around porch like the ones you see in old pictures: a wide one with round columns. Inside was very cozy, an old-fashioned house with a sitting parlor, lots of wood work details, crown moldings etc. We lived on the main floor; one fellow lived on the lower floor and Markus, who became my friend, on the upper level.

We enjoyed visiting, going out in the woods, having barbecues and dinners. He always seemed to sense when I was having difficult days and would say, "I think you should make a lunch and we should go for a drive in the bush." He knew quiet was something that was good for me; he could see it and we did it often.

I enjoyed the house and neighborhood. The location was really good; I could walk to town, and all around there was great pedestrian paths. Phoebe and I would go for long walks every day; I could walk to everything I needed if I wasn't feeling up to driving, and it was great having Markus close by if I needed help.

Tuesday, May 17, 2016

I hate when I can't find the words I am looking for, or when I am talking to someone and I'm just gone in the middle of the conversation. So many things are different: like I send messages to my friends that make no sense, time means nothing anymore. For instance, yesterday afternoon I could not remember what happened to the morning or what I did. I have reminders for everything. Another example: a couple of days ago I wanted to bring up my credit card on my computer to see the statements. I set it all up and put the username and password into my notes. Today I went to my notes, put the information in and it was not correct. I wrote it down wrong which means writing things down is not always helpful. It's like what my brain is wanting to do is coming out scrambled.

*****

One day, September 16th, 2016, something happened inside my brain. I tried to explain it later, couldn't really make anyone understand, perhaps I still don't totally understand. I was at home having a normal sort of day; I took my dog for her walks as I usually did. Sometime in the afternoon something caused me to panic or go into fight or flight mode, I am not even sure how to label it. I was just going.

Markus apparently tried to stop me, he couldn't; off I went, somehow, and ended up in Kelowna. I was almost to the bridge and I wondered, *why am I here, where am I going?* I turned around, headed back towards Vernon, turned around again, back towards the bridge, I am not sure how many times I did that or what made me stop in a parking lot. I think I decided to text Barb (my travelling companion) and pulled over to write. From there, things were hazy. Barb said she knew by my answers, they were all garbled, that I was not okay. She phoned me, I am not sure what time that was, I know she asked me where I was, where I was going. She talked me into staying put, then talked me into getting a coffee.

Eventually my mind shifted, she had changed the focus of my brain…I was then able to get home by 10 PM after witnessing an accident. My car was damaged when the very large deer that jumped into the path of the truck in front of me slid under the front of my car. My car was still drivable, his truck was totaled and we waited for police and tow trucks.

Transcript of Barb's and Chrissy's text messages: edited for clarity by Barb.

5:46 PM

Chrissy – I have been going in and out of Kelowna…frozen, can't seem to go anywhere, no confidence in my ability to manage it.

Barb – What? Head home, that's safest. Do we need to come get you? Are you driving? Pull over and message me back!

Chrissy – Okay, I'm pulled over.

Barb – Are you okay and where are you? Do you need us to come get you?

Chrissy – No, I am just teary, drove into Kelowna, almost panicked, couldn't cross the bridge, drove back towards airport, turned around tried again, then thought maybe if I just made a reservation down south then it would be okay, couldn't do that, headed back towards airport, back into Kelowna, makes me sad.

Barb – It's okay, you're safe, that's what matters. Where are you now? It's also Friday rush hour.

Chrissy – In the parking lot across from mall. Markus is really going to think I've lost my mind.
Barb – That doesn't matter.

Chrissy – I feel really stupid

Barb – Don't, just head home.

Chrissy – I am going to drive so will text next time I stop.

Barb – If you wait, traffic will lighten up, go have a coffee.

Chrissy – Yes, good idea.

Barb – Okay, keep me posted.

Chrissy – I'm at Whitespot.

Barb – Okay, take a break.

Chrissy – Will have a bite and coffee, regroup.
Barb – Good idea. You're okay, that's what matters.

Chrissy – Yup.

7:08 PM
Chrissy – Just hanging out between Lake Country and Kelowna.

Barb – Message me when you're home please. Try to get home before dark.

Chrissy – Yup, don't worry I'll be fine Yes I will start that way, now it's raining.

Barb – I won't sleep till I know you're home.

7:48 PM
Chrissy – Sitting at Highway 97 College Way, guy hit deer, deer hit me. No one hurt, go to bed, all is okay.

Barb – Good grief! How's your car? You okay?

Chrissy – Goodnight

Markus was beside himself with worry. He and Barb texted, but he struggled to comprehend what was happening to me…he still struggles, but he tries. We arranged, because I saw Markus so often (nearly daily at that time), that he was to text or phone Barb if he was not sure how to help me. They have, on a few occasions, done this. Through the winter months Barb was always great with gentle reminders…like, "Hon, we're going here," never making me feel bad, just always helping make it okay. I knew within myself things were continuing to change.

Sunday, October 9, 2016

Wow, I haven't posted here for a long time, partly because I could not always figure out how to navigate the site and also because I decided I really needed to focus solely on getting well, doing all I could to help myself. So, Electro-Proscope (electrical currents to stimulate blood flow to my brain) treatments, physiotherapy, massage therapy, cranial sacral treatments, palates, walking, biking, and learning how to breathe properly, all part of the plan. I watch my eating habits, sleeping habits, rid my life of all that can or does cause me stress. It is imperative that my blood pressure stay stable; when it goes up, I am in trouble. I am learning to look at the changes, manage things differently. I allow my body to have what it needs when it needs it instead of feeling all obligations must be met and pushing, pushing, pushing.

I am trying to figure out how I can work again. Then I question why I put so much pressure on myself, thinking that if I am not productive, I am somehow lacking. In fact, I work full time to stay as healthy as I can. I am thankful that those around me understand. Yet in the back of my mind, I know I could still be productive, that I have lots to offer.

I am trying to figure out the next step, waiting for more specialist appointments then hoping to put a plan together. I am learning to live in the unknown. It's not always comfortable but I am becoming better at it each day.

It is Canadian Thanksgiving. I am thankful that I still function as well as I do. I am most grateful and thankful to have the friends and family around me who help me live in this new reality. I know it is not always easy for them, I know at times it is scary for all of us but through laughter and tears they truly are my life's blessings. So today on this beautiful sunny Thanksgiving weekend, I will just breathe and be grateful.

*****

As time progressed, my needs were changing. I needed a calmer household. My roommate's and my lifestyles were no longer as cohesive as they had once been. By Christmas 2016, I had started packing, planning to move the end of March. Unfortunately, it became apparent after I came home from being away over the holidays (Markus took me to see my kids and to an Oilers and Canucks game in Edmonton for New Year's Eve) that it was time for me to move. I had to look after my health and well-being first and foremost. Life was changing for her also.

By the end of January, 2017, I had put my things into storage, made arrangements to rent Brent and Kay's little suite for a few months as I was going to do some housing-sitting on and off until the end of June then for the full months of July and August. This was going to allow me to see how I was adjusting to the new medications and find the appropriate housing. This has been a good decision; it has allowed me to again focus on my health, working with the doctors, having a safe place to be as I work through the medications building in my system. The doctors are helping me get a proper plan into place going forward.

Chapter Five

Garnered from 'Chrissy's Journey' on Facebook.

Tuesday, February 21, 2017

Today is an important day; I had an appointment with all my doctors. I have vascular dementia and they have been trialing me on the medication Aricept. It has been producing fairly good results. Tomorrow I will start the final increase in the dosage and will remain on it for the unforeseeable future. It is also important because the decision has been made by them that my nursing career is over. I say this with a heavy heart as I truly loved my work and treasured all those I met along the way. I love the people I have worked with who have become like family to me.

I do understand, however, that I cannot put anyone at risk. I know I have talked about it being a possibility and hung on to the hope that something would change; maybe I would wake up and it would all have been a dream but, in my heart, I know that is not the case. I also have chosen to continue looking for the silver lining in all of this, I am sure there will be some, there has already been some.

This is a journey into the unknown in so many ways. Yet, because of my chosen career, I know a lot more than most people do about what is happening to me. I have always said knowledge is power…today I wonder if that is necessarily true…but again deep down I know it is. My focus will now be on building a new life, a different life, so I can remain independent for as long as I possibly can.

Right now, the medication allows me to remain fairly high functioning. Some days I have to forgo my plans just to manage. I hope to spend this next year with many family and friends and it may be difficult for others to comprehend why I am as I am now. Please know that it is okay to talk to me about it and ask questions. I will answer as honestly as I can. I hope perhaps I can, at some point, help someone along the way by sharing my journey. My doctors are encouraging me to do some speaking about living with dementia to people who work with and live with clients. So, finally, I would like to say thank you all for being part of my journey, remember to live each day, love each day and be grateful each day.

Thursday, February 23, 2017

So many things are different now; I didn't even realize, until I started on the Aricept, how in so many ways I was not managing as well as I had thought. For sure I had friends around me who compensated for me. Bless their hearts. My family and friends ensured that nothing totally devastating happened. I have come to the realization that if I am to write and try to help others along this journey it is going to take some brutal honesty on my part. In a sense it's like taking the mask off, being real, being vulnerable.

If I am honest, I can say it is at night, or in the wee hours of the morning when my mind and body are at rest that I allow the fears to enter. Yes, I am afraid, terrified actually, afraid of the day I can no longer take care of myself, afraid of the day I have to give up driving, afraid of ending up in care (I have decided that can't and won't happen). There are many times I wish I wasn't alone and I mean that in the sense of having a partner, the one who hugs you in the night when you have tears, the one you can take the mask off around. Then I realize that I also don't think I would have wanted him to endure this journey I am now on.

I always hear people say, "You're so lucky: no one to pick up after, no one to cook for etc." Hum, being alone is tough no matter how many great friends you have and I truly am blessed in that regard. But at the end of the day, I am still alone. Does that make this journey more difficult? I am not sure. Living with illness, no matter what type, is difficult.

Most illnesses however allow us treatment plans, projected outcomes. This disease does not. It will inflict itself on my life at whatever pace it likes in whichever ways it likes. It has forever changed who I am. Oh, there are still parts of me that shine through on good days. On those days the spunk, the sparkle are still there. Not with the same intensity but they are there. The new medication has allowed for that and I am grateful. So, most days you see the me that smiles and says, "I'm great" or "I'm fine," because that's what I need to do to manage. But sometimes I have to be allowed to take the mask off.

Friday, February 24, 2017

So, it's little things that I must do: every night before I go to sleep, I have questions I ask myself, like, "Where am I?" Sometimes it takes me a little while to remember. Every morning I have a list of questions I ask myself upon waking, like, "What is my name, where do I live?" etc. I do this because it's how I check in to see how my brain is. Is today the day I will wake up to find out I have lost a little more of myself and my world? I feel grateful every day when I can answer those questions.

Information: it's not that I have forgotten; it is like my brain has taken memories and put them in a filing cabinet. Sometimes the filing cabinet is locked and what's inside is unavailable, other times the cabinet opens up and the information flows wonderfully and sometimes it just takes a long time to find the right file. When I can't find it, the frustration sets in. I may get angry. I am not angry at anyone, just the situation, because I know that I still know what I want, I just can't retrieve it. Sometimes that creates sadness; sometimes it triggers an element of panic or anxiety because I know I am trapped within the confines of my damaged brain.

The doctors know that I had a very deep stroke on that day at work two years ago. They also know that I have to focus on keeping cholesterol low, blood pressure low, create a low-stress life. All these things are to manage the risks of another major stroke. The dementia is a result of many factors, but the stroke brought it to what it is today. I will smile, I will take in the day, I will be grateful for all that I can still manage and do.

Saturday, February 25, 2017

Yesterday was a day plagued by side effects from the increase of medications which will come and go and can take up to 12 weeks to level out. I was outside for a bit but came home: now lying low watching Netflix. I'm so cold from the inside out nothing can warm me up. I've got headache and bad muscle cramps; these will likely all go away later.

I am struggling a little with the whole never-work-again thing. Funny how much emphasis we all put on our careers when in reality we should put more into our personal passions and the people we care about. It is an adjustment having the hope of returning to work now gone. But as with all things, I am a realist and I will find other ways to still feel productive. I have always been a strong advocate for people with dementia. Maybe I will find a way to have an even stronger voice.

Taking care of myself first is also a difficult lesson. Because people think I look great, they also think there is nothing wrong with me. They see me on my good days; they don't see the days I am sitting at home and can't figure out what I am supposed to be doing or the days I have things to do but go to the wrong places. I am teaching myself not to panic, to sit and breathe, to wait,

wait, wait for clarity to come…waiting for my brain to release information I am so desperately wanting in those moments.

Sunday, February 26, 2017

I have always been a very decisive person…making a decision then getting on with it; except now my brain doesn't want to make a decision. Another frustration. Today I will challenge my brain to start building a plan and putting it on paper.

Monday, February 27, 2017

I always write in the mornings; things become more difficult as the day wears on. If I am trying to write or work with numbers, I know them in my brain but on paper they end up as something totally different; it's frustrating and makes so many things more challenging.

I am trying to allow myself the right to grieve for a life gone and at the same time find a way to embrace this new life and to balance and shift between the two. I am still alive, many, many parts of me are still here, but I am acutely aware of the ones which are not. I always had such a sense of knowing 'that I could manage,' that 'I would be okay,' knowing what I wanted. Now I know none of those things for sure. Yet, somehow, I have managed to make some decisions for myself, it just takes longer.

My sleep patterns are a mess. Part of that is the disease itself; the other part is the medication. Both affect a person with dementia. My brain is tired and wants to sleep so some days I sleep from 8:30 PM until 7 the following morning, some days I sleep in spurts of half hours then I have to get up and move around, sometimes I nap for longer periods then need to eat something. It's not anything I can control.

Tuesday, February 28, 2017

I used to never like solitude, enjoyed having a houseful and socialized a lot. I am now much quieter, my voice that fought hard for people now whispers. I am not very social anymore, although, sometimes I long for one of those big get-togethers I used to execute. It is difficult; I am only 57 years old! Because of the type of dementia I have, because of my age, I am very aware of what's happening to me. I find I am in a personal struggle to ensure I am not isolating myself and at the same time allowing the solitude that is part of the disease be enjoyable. The 'me' I am most comfortable with; that's the one I fight hard to hang on to.

My lawyer and I sat down and tackled the daunting task of getting things in order….my will rewritten first. I wonder if people realize they should have one…they are so important…not because of money or stuff but because when someone dies, it is such a difficult task to get through the day never mind trying to navigate all that has to be done. A will simplifies many things for those left behind. By writing a will, you are actually giving those you left in charge of your affairs the gift of easing an otherwise daunting task. Wills should be reviewed from time to time so they are current. Mine is now current. I also have all my power of attorney papers in order.

There is always so many issues around a person's ability to make their own decisions and about whether they are able to convey clearly what their wishes are when they have been diagnosed with dementia. We need to have things done in legal form. I intend, in the next little while, to add a living testimonial to my portfolio so when the time comes there can be no misinterpretation of what I want.

I have witnessed time and time again, family, caregivers, nursing staff, all insisting that a person is fed even when it is clear this is no longer a viable action. I believe it is done because people have the need 'to do something' when clearly a person doesn't want any more to be done. Many times the body is trying to shut down and we are forcing it to do unnatural things during that process. Really, we should be giving them comfort, respect, relief from pain and allowing their bodies to do what is natural.

We have become a society that doesn't want to accept death. Our own belief systems take over, our selfishness wants to hang on to someone rather than give them the gift of allowing them to die as they want to and enjoying their last days. This causes much distress.

There is a saying that I love; it is 'If you love me, let me go.' Loving someone enough to be selfless is a beautiful gift to give someone; I know because I've done it, with my husband, and then my mother – their way, on their terms. I moved mountains so that could happen and I would do it over again a million times.

So, I have very precise health care directives, I do not want to be spoon fed, I do not want anything more than fluid if I want that; if I can't swallow anymore then only good mouth care, and keep my lips moist, no feeding tubes.

I want nursing staff to put in lines to administer medications, I don't want someone deciding I look comfortable and skipping a dose because they don't want to disturb me. Even if I am asleep, I want my medications administered at the times and dosages prescribed, without question!

I have seen how long it takes to make a patient comfortable again once a dose is missed and we have to play catch-up. My doctor can throw every medicine at his disposal at me to keep me calm, quiet and out of pain, and I want no one to interfere with that.

I don't want to be forced to be up because it's easier on the staff. Ah yes, I know they will say it's better for the person so they don't get pneumonia or bed sores. Sorry, that doesn't cut it for me. When I reach the stage when I can no longer feed myself, it's time to call it a day. Quite honestly, getting pneumonia would be a blessing, a peaceful way to die.

I will decide the day I stop taking all my medicines, hoping for a stroke or heart failure. I already have a date in mind. No, I do not have a death wish, I was already given the death sentence with my diagnosis, I work very hard to stay as well as I can and will continue to do so for as long as I can. When that is no longer possible, then everything stops, and eventually I will no longer be able to feed myself and the end stages can be allowed to happen.

End-of-life decisions are something most people won't talk about leaving; loved ones often have to make decisions that are best done by the dying person. I have never wanted to be a burden to anyone, never want to be. I believe God gave our bodies the tools to shut down when He is ready for us. I had someone say if I don't allow those things to be done then I am playing God. Actually, I believe I am letting God do His work the way He wants to.

My DNR and all my health care paperwork are posted in an envelope so that any first responders would see it and have it to take to the hospital to ensure my wishes are known. My doctor and I review it every few months.

Friday, March 3, 2017

I am in Kamloops visiting friends and colleagues from my time working here. I like the blue skies; I like that it is not so socked in and gray (In the winter, the Okanagan Valley has its own cloud cover which keeps in the warmth but can get dreary). Yesterday, I was trying to do some shopping with my girlfriend and we ended up leaving the store because it proved too challenging for me. I felt overwhelmed, frustrated, and angry at myself. Later trying to do some things on her computer, things that I was always able to do without even thinking about them, proved to be very challenging and frustrating. This is the first glimpse of my latest struggles my girlfriend, Wendy, has seen firsthand. We adjusted what we were doing; she enlisted her son to help me with my computer project. I am grateful that I have friends that are doing all they can to support me. It's all those little tasks that become huge challenges, the very things I have always taken for granted. I see my shortfalls, I compensate for a lot of them, I change how and when I tackle things, some things I no longer tackle.

Monday, March 6, 2017

After spending time this morning doing my writing, I was scrolling through my Facebook page and this article popped up. I found it relevant, and an interesting read. Dr. Gary Breitbart performed three randomized, controlled experiments using meaning-centered (finding meaning in living) psychotherapy. When he analyzed the results with his colleagues, he saw the therapy had been transformative. By the end of the eight sessions, the patients' attitudes toward life and death had changed. They were less hopeless and anxious about the prospect of death than they were before they began the program. They no longer wanted to die. Their spiritual wellbeing improved. They reported a higher quality of life. And, of course, they found life to be more meaningful. These effects not only persisted over time – they actually got stronger. When Breitbart followed up with one group of patients two months later, he found that their reports of meaning and spiritual wellbeing had increased, while their feelings of anxiety, hopelessness, and desire for death had decreased.

The time between diagnosis and death, he found, presents an opportunity for 'extraordinary growth.' One woman, for example, was initially devastated by her diagnosis of colon cancer – but after enrolling in the meaning-therapy program, she realized, "I didn't have to work so hard to find the meaning in life. It was being handed to me everywhere I looked." And that realization ultimately brought her – and Breitbart's other patients – some measure of peace and consolation as they faced life's final challenge.

I know the stats show that once diagnosed with Vascular Dementia a person usually lives 5 to 8 years. That would put me at 66. We also know that people diagnosed young usually die of heart or stroke, not the actual dementia. That is something I can accept. That in fact would be a blessing. I don't want to linger on in a world where I am trapped inside my brain. I hope that I will be able to manage to live independently for the better amount of my given years. Time goes so fast; we are already into another March of my remaining years. There is still much I want to do, see, experience.

I was visiting with one of my lovely friends yesterday and we were discussing taking opportunities when they come along. She understands how short life truly is and she said something that I feel is so true and so much of what I try to express but can't so I will quote her. "I would rather live with the regret of taking an opportunity that failed to work out, than to live with the regret of not taking the opportunity at all."

I am trying to take opportunities, taking life all in, enjoying the scenery, enjoying all those who are important to me. I want to laugh, be silly, cry, all of it, and time is going so fast. I don't want pity, I don't want sympathy, I can accept the hand dealt to me, I can even look for and find many blessings. Does it suck sometimes? Yes, it makes me sad. But I don't and won't let the negative things be my focus. Today might be the best day I have left. In the blink of an eye five years have gone by. Now if only I could remember what those important things were that I am supposed to be discussing at my doctor's appointment Tuesday!

Tuesday, March 7, 2017

It truly makes such a difference for people if they have doctors they can talk to, doctors who take the time to listen, who talk TO them, not AT them. Kindness and compassion go a long way to help a patient's overall wellbeing. I am aware of how many people do not have their own physician. I cannot imagine what it must be like for them. This journey for me would be unbearable without the support, help, knowledge and consistency in the care I receive. This week has been a struggle; my blood pressure and heart rate have been too high.

My visit to Kamloops was wonderful, was great to visit; however, it was done in small doses and having the ability to just BE when necessary made it a great way to have an enjoyable time without tiring my brain too much. I definitely have learned that I can no longer manage too many things coming at me all at the same time; I cannot process things or multitask like I used to. Perhaps that is why solitude and isolation are so prominent in people with dementia. We can, in the quiet, hear our own voices and thoughts. They are accessible, no overwhelming outside distractions scattering them.

Today has been a totally devastating day...my doctors visit confirmed I did in fact suffer another TIA (tiny stroke) a few days ago. Nothing can be done, I do everything I can, they do all they can, it is part of my vascular disease which then impacts my vascular dementia. So next week I have an appointment with a couple of doctors which will be 1 hour and 45 minutes in length. There will be lots looked at, support services put into place, living arrangements made, the list goes on. I have told people that I knew the day would come but was not expecting today to be that day.

It won't be long before they pull my license. My years of driving will come to an end, likely by late fall or maybe sooner but I am truly hoping to drive at least into fall...the queen of road trips will be no more...so as much as I want to sit and cry, I will not. Until then I will be going on as many adventures as I can, as often as I can, here, there, everywhere, anywhere...I would truly love one last big road trip, but if I can't make that happen, I will do as many smaller ones as I have in me. I will be out to make memories. If I get lost, it will be an adventure, if I forget where I am going, I will just be happy to be somewhere. Today hurts but tomorrow I will again smile and say, "Forward I go."

Book Two
Perseverance

Chapter Six

Thursday, March 9, 2017

Yesterday no writing, just a day of doing normal things, a day of reflection, an enjoyable day, letting my body just BE, no pushing through anything. I enjoyed my lunch out, visiting, talking about normal things, families, kids, jobs, so great. On my way home I did a little grocery shopping, a hair trim and an afternoon walk. This evening I pulled together journal entries that I began two years ago when all this started. I wanted to organize a presentation that I can use for giving talks and found it a challenge to put together. Still, it did feel good to be productive.

Funny, reading back, the one thing that stood out for me was the large gaps in time between when I was journaling and when I was not. I tried to figure out why: was I just too sick, just forgot or was too exhausted? I don't know. However, it is remarkable to me when reading some of the posts that I actually am still here…or that I am functioning at all…I guess I am not done yet!

I found one thing I wrote recently that I will add here: There are so many things that need to be done differently…for example caretakers wonder why they have behavioral problems with those who have dementia. I can tell you. Although our minds may not be what they once were and maybe we can't always tell you what we need or want, we are aware of much. We like to walk, we like to be in the fresh air, we want to dig in the dirt and muck in the flowers. Maybe an outdoor nursing station is required. Take all those dementia units outside and forget the bingo and exercises. Spend as much of the day as you can outside with us, every day. Let us nap, eat, and wander with you.

When you lock us up in such confined spaces you instill panic, you instill anger, frustration and fear…you will get the behavior problems, the lashing out, the violence…because you have created it. Yes, there will always be a small number of people who, with this or any other disease, will naturally have violent or anger tendencies. But you will not have it to such a degree. I know I will become your worst nightmare if I am confined. If we changed this one thing, quality of life would be better and interesting enough for both patient and worker. In the long run this would save vast amounts of money. We would eat better, sleep better, not need so many behavioral medications. Staff would have less stress, less sick time and work in a healthier, environment.

Friday, March 10, 2017

This week I have struggled with small things, going downtown instead of going to the doctor because I forgot, not remembering if I actually bought something, if I did what did I do with it? I wrote appointments down multiple times because I forgot I had written them down and wrote them all on different dates so didn't know which, if any, were right. Being on the Aricept helps but does not eliminate those things and it is worse right now due to the TIA late last week. Trying to follow and comprehend simple instructions also became an issue. Being able to laugh about it becomes a necessary skill. It's the only way I can get through it all. Having amazing people around me who give phone calls, texts, gentle reminders, help. I am so very grateful my treasure chest of life is full of treasures. Love them all.

Saturday, March 11, 2017

Earlier today, I had coffee with two very dear friends, Barb and Karen (nurse friends). Thank you both for your honesty about what it's like to be my friend, walk this journey and not be afraid to share the laughter, tears and fears. We talked openly and honestly about the fact that I want the 'right to die with dignity.' It is a very personal choice; it is not a choice anyone makes lightly. I have knowledge and insight into this disease, knowledge the majority with the illness do not have, I know this disease inside out and outside in. It was my calling, it was my work, I have held, cried and laughed, and been with so many as they take their final breaths!

I will not go into any type of long-term care, private or public. I know so, so many loving, kind, caring, and compassionate people who truly do amazing jobs in these facilities, they truly love those they care for, those people are truly a gift to all. But I also know there are many who should not be working on those types of units, in those positions, whether they are the RN, LPN, Care Aid, housekeepers, food service workers, whatever. The system allows them to continue working long beyond what is acceptable. I have always been a loud voice for this to change.

We need to move workers if they are not suited. There are many types of care, but this type of care – dementia care – not only needs special and ongoing training, it takes a different type of personality, those truly capable of providing some sense of quality to those with the illness. I know the system is not set up for that, the bureaucratic nightmare does not allow those amazing people to do their jobs, to be heard. They are the ones who know what's needed, they are the ones who could give us the best quality of life possible. It's always about the budget, the money, the regulations. If decision makers listened to the people who truly are great at what they do, if they spent the money on building proper facilities, revamped existing ones with those workers' input, then we would have a facility I could consider. If you moved people working those units who should not be with our vulnerable, then maybe, just maybe I would change my mind.

In my conversations I have heard more than once that doctors are required to do no harm. But harm is being done by modern medicine every day. We keep people alive long after it is reasonable. If we took away all the machines, all the force feeding, our bodies would do what they are meant to do – shut down naturally. We don't educate people to understand dying, to help them accept the process.

When we force people to live beyond all reasonable situations it is out of our own personal selfish needs. I get it, wow how I get it. I was 47 years old when I had to let my husband go. I had to be selfless; I had to move beyond what I wanted to what he wanted and what was best for him.

So, no I will not go into a facility where I will be caged in an area that has a hallway 30 feet long, where I can't go outside and wander and sit because that's where I feel good that's where I have peace. I will not be forced to eat whether I want to or not, wake up, get up, go to bed when and how it works best for 'the system.' No, I will not go into care. If you think people like me don't have the right to choose, I suggest you take up residence for a month then tell me what your choice would be.

Monday, March 13, 2017

I wish that I knew someone who could sit down and draw the picture that is inside my head. It would show a facility set up as it should be for dementia patients. I don't have the ability to do that. We shouldn't be in institutions. Society call them 'care homes' because that makes people feel better but truly they are simply institutions. The medical community paint pretty pictures for those on the outside but, honestly, the facilities are failing. Bureaucrats worry so much about the rules and regulations that the system has stopped allowing the patients to have a place to thrive.

Thursday, March 16, 2017

Did you know that during WWII the enemy locked prisoners in a small space then created all kinds of noise until they would break? We take dementia patients, lock them in a small area (like a 150 foot by five-foot corridor) to pace, no windows, poor lighting, lots of noise, cleaning machines, carts, trolleys, dollies, televisions, people's voices, and we are shocked when their behavior turns bad. Hmmmm. And don't you dare tell me it's not that bad. Don't you dare. Because I know! As I lay in the quiet and say my prayers I ask, "Dear Lord, if I must have this illness then please, let something take me and don't ever allow me to end up in long term care or the Dementia Unit."

Six months ago I started using headphones a lot. I had never liked them but I bought a good set of wireless headphones and now I practically live in them. They allow me to listen, to focus without the background noise. It is also why all summer long my preference was to be out in the country, out in the woods, where the only noise was nature, birds singing, leaves rustling, it's when I feel my best, it's when I function best.

Friday, March 17, 2017

I have an event at 9 AM today except I didn't write what it was or where, so I will be late…ha ha. Sometimes you have to laugh at life. It's 7:53, I am still in my pajamas which rarely, and I do mean rarely, happens, enjoying my coffee and just being. I should be out for my morning walk already, but I have the whole day so this morning I will be lazy. Brenda says they are doing music therapy in care homes now and setting residents up with iPads. I truly hope the care givers realize they have to play music their patrons enjoy, not what the workers think they will enjoy and, this is important, that they get them wireless headphones. Ear buds will aggravate most of them and any wires will cause them frustrations. Yesterday I realized that I suddenly feel very small in a very large world. It was a lovely day. I do have happiness, peacefulness, laughter in part because all of the things one would normally stress about are irrelevant for me, not important enough to take up space or time in my day. My sister and I have a trip planned for June to Niagara Falls. Yesterday she wondered if I felt up to it. Heck yes sister, I am very able bodied, I will take it all in, we will laugh, we will have fun it will be a grand adventure, and in the event you and I don't get to do another, those photos I will take will be something I have to look at and in my heart I will know I had fun. I intend to pack in as much as I can feasibly manage, with those I care about, while I can laugh at the confusion and mistakes because they will all make the journey more memorable.

Saturday, March 18, 2017

It feels like the medications are taking effect in the last couple days, the veil lifting. I am in awe of my brain; I am in awe of how little control we actually have in our lives. I believe in the lose it or use it philosophy. I took courses and learned something new every year. I did crosswords, Sudoku, Luminosity all those healthy grain things for years. But there are some things we do not have control over.

Sunday, March 19, 2017

The thick fog surrounding my brain is light, almost non-existent this morning, a good indication that the Aricept is building in my system and working. Also, it helps that I walked 7.68 miles yesterday. Walking improves things for me each day; perhaps the walking keeps the blood flow to my brain topped up! When the flow is low the symptoms are worse; the fog thickens, settles in, like closing room-darkening drapes. That is why I believe my physiotherapy and Pilates is also important. I was going four days a week, that was giving me the most benefit but I can no longer afford that so I go once a week. I hope to somehow manage the four days a week again. I also have bio-cranial treatments and have received bio electro treatments. Today because the fog is lifted, I intend to squeeze every ounce out of the day; today the me I have always been has been allowed to surface.

Wow, I knew a word I needed yesterday but it took over an hour on the computer this morning to find it again. What is the word and the relevance, you ask? The word is 'concept.' I have lost all concept of time, it is unimportant; I am suddenly truly living in the moment. One minute it is six in the morning, the next it's ten at night. Where all those hours go doesn't seem important. I am happy to just BE.

I have learned to compensate for a lot of things that are more challenging now. For instance, it's like words are on a conveyer belt, the conveyer belt is set at the lowest speed and each falls off at the end one by one until finally the last word falls to complete the sentence. I am still so high functioning that most who meet me or talk to me don't even know that I am one of the many walking wounded: the Dementia Secret. I choose not to keep it a secret; I choose to share. I share to make my life bearable.

Tuesday, March 21, 2017

Yesterday was a comedy of errors. Messed thing up at the gas station, the guy had to come out to help me reset it all, he was so kind. At the bank I couldn't remember my password. By the time I was done grocery shopping at 1 PM I was exhausted. Good thing I have a sense of humor about it all.

I had a short visit with my friend Sharon. She said there is such a peacefulness about me these days; it's like I am on a different plane. I feel a peacefulness that I cannot explain at a time when I could be stressed, scared, angry. I feel calm, at ease. I used to be very hard on myself if I made a mistake. Now the mistakes happen but I don't get upset by it. Mistakes can be fixed and I just accept this is the new me and laugh, another one of those silver linings.

Wednesday, March 22, 2017

Yesterday I walked over 10 miles total, so in six days I walked 48 miles. Love walking, love being in the fresh air and it's so good for helping my sleep. I let myself think about the important things. I switched to the Credit Union today because they are readier to put things in place that will help me maintain my independence; the more things are simplified the longer I will manage on my own.

The next big thing is my car. I am thinking about that a lot lately. Driving is such a big part of who I am. It's becoming more important that I decide when and how to part with my car than about having a car. I know that decision is coming within months; it's the reality of having strokes, no matter how small, on a continual basis. I realize family and friends watching will all have differing opinions of what I should do, but the fact is it will be less sad if I choose rather than have someone tell me.

Friday, March 24, 2017

Yesterday was really great. I spent the day with Dawn (my half-sister), lots of laughter, a few tears, but a great visit. I truly have learned to enjoy the moments with those I care about.

Sunday, March 26, 2017

I had a great conversation with my sister-in-law Kay. I always enjoy our conversations; always find them insightful and something she said stuck with me. She told me that she felt that I often seem lonely, which was an interesting observation. I have never thought of myself as being lonely. But she is quite right I am lonely, I am lonely for the life I had, the person I was. Some days it's like nothing has changed, the me I always knew emerges. Then she slips away and I am lonely. I don't expect it will make any sense to anyone else but does make sense to me. I miss always striving to do more, learn more, help more. Even though I have a peacefulness that I never had before, I also at times have this loneliness because I am lonely for a part of me that has vanished.

Monday, March 27, 2017

It feels as though the medication may have finally reached a level that gives me more clarity…yippee! Today I am heading to the Coast with my friend June. I'm going to spend the week down there, a night at Harrison Hot Springs, a night at Steveston (yum, fish and chips) and a few nights with my sister-in-law Christa. I also hope the sun will shine a little while we are down there, maybe all the trees and tulips and daffodils will be out. Spring seems to be really taking its time this year; maybe it means we will be rewarded with a lovely long fall. I will take a lot of pictures. All my pictures will become my memory. If I don't remember each adventure, at least I will remember, when I look at the pictures, that I was happy. I can't be locked up in a unit somewhere. To not be able to walk, smell the rain, feel the snow and sun would kill me faster than anything.

Wednesday, March 29, 2017

Yesterday we travelled from Harrison Hot Springs to Richmond and the rain came down in a true West Coast downpour all day. Strange, my love of shopping has vanished. I have always loved IKEA; I have spent many happy hours marveling at their brilliance when it comes to selling things that function. But in the store I struggled with noise, too many people and an extended phone call from Interior Health so we left early. At Steveston I was so happy to hear the sea gulls, smell the ocean air then eat fabulous fish and chips. June dropped me off in Maple Ridge then went to her Aunt and Uncle's and I had a good night's sleep at Christa's. Today we will just enjoy a quiet day of visiting; it will be good for both of us.

Thursday, March 30, 2017

The birds are singing, the rain has stopped and I am hoping for a good long walk today. I miss my walks; it really affects my sleep. I also have fewer headaches if I walk. I made a lovely dinner for us last night and we had a great visit. The visits have had to be short with her needing to be in bed in between but the times she was able to be up were so good. She has had a massive dose of chemicals to kill her cancers and is hopefully fighting her way back to health. We both struggle with giving up so much independence, asking for and

59

receiving help. After spending our lives looking after ourselves, it seems too early. We laughed about it.

Friday, March 31, 2017

Yesterday my niece Elisabeth was here for a visit; it was nice chatting with her about stress, pressure and learning about self-care. I am glad she is learning about it now, not in 20 years. So many my age suffer the consequences of giving our all to care for those around us and neglecting to take care of ourselves. I am sure that my Vascular Dementia, although partly my genetic makeup, was exacerbated due to high levels for stress for long periods of time.

Chapter Seven

Saturday, April 1, 2017

I forgot to take my CPP (continuous positive airway pressure) machine when I went away, it makes a huge difference for me, I mustn't forget it in the future. I have all of my permanent disability things finalized so I officially will not work for Interior Health BC again. While I was gone, I took Christa to the senior's center where she volunteers. It's a small but lovely group. I had coffee with them; one lady was 103 and still motoring without any assistance. Another was ninety, delightful, with a great sense of humor. We shared a few good laughs together. Still, it left me deeply saddened, I miss my job, miss doing what I love.

My first presentation on 'Living with Dementia' will take place on April 11th at 2 PM. I am excited and nervous all at the same time. In doing this I have to allow myself to be vulnerable, to allow others to see the pieces and parts that I often write about, but people don't usually see. I can hope I am having one of my really good days. It took me a very long time to put together the presentation. Thankfully my brother-in-law checked it over, tidied it up so it was exactly as I wanted it.

I also had a call from the Alzheimer's in Kelowna. The woman comes to Vernon once a month and wants to meet with me so that will likely be in April as well. I am looking forward to getting back into my walking routine today.

It is daunting trying to navigate applications such as the Canada Disability Pension forms when you have dementia. There truly should be a simplified way for these things to be done but it feels good to know that I was able to get through it without a lot of assistance, small victories.

Monday, April 3, 2017

I woke up at 4 AM thinking how good a hot cup of coffee would be. Oh dear, no cream for my coffee! So that's what I went to the store for yesterday! I wrote it in my notes but forgot to look at them. I used to drink my coffee black years ago so it won't hurt.

Tuesday, April 4, 2017

I am trying to find an apartment that will accept my little dog; I can't imagine having to part with her. She is all I have left and the thought of letting her go is harder than dealing with any other aspect of this illness; it brings me to my knees. She is my companion; she takes care of me more than I take care of her. I also have to look for housing that is in town, within walking distance to everything I need and safe. I feel like I'm doing life in reverse: the uncertainty is known so I have to dismantle my life then try to figure out which piece to remake first and how fast. I truly will be glad when my housing situation is settled. It is the final major piece that will allow me to see into the future with greater ease.

Wednesday, April 5, 2017

Last night I was trying to remember something and I had a good chuckle because I thought, oh well, it won't matter for long because I will soon forget that I have forgotten!

Yesterday I walked on the rail trail for three hours and remembered as a young girl how I used to walk the railway tracks to get home from school or to get to town.

I will at some point have to give up my driver's license. The doctor keeps having this conversation with me. Looking back, I remembered how many people didn't think it was a great idea to buy my Mini Cooper. Many thought I should wait and buy something more practical then buy it when I actually retired. I am so grateful that I followed my heart and my gut and got my car. It was my lifelong dream to have one, I have enjoyed many road trips with it the last few years and I am hoping to complete a couple more. Yesterday I had the top down for the first time this year, I felt so happy to have the fresh air on my face, it made me want to drive away and just keep driving. I have fulfilled that lifelong dream. When the time comes I will let it go with grace, dignity, and sadness. Giving up driving will be difficult but maybe a little less difficult because I already fulfilled a dream.

Friday, April 7, 2017

I want to talk to the business manager at BMW today about my car, best time to sell, what I might get for it then I will be able to make a decision from what I learn. Here's hoping for some good news on that front.

I believe that the weather we have here is not good for people with dementia just like it is known to affect people prone to headaches and migraines. I believe the amount of low-pressure days we have make the brain fog worse. I'll plan vacations for those times when we have the most: from mid-December till end of April. Boy, isn't that a big dream?

Saturday, April 8, 2017

Five hours of good sleep, and I wake up and realize I missed two appointments this last week and double-booked appointments for the coming week. Oh well, they can be rebooked and rescheduled. I must write myself a big note to fix all this on Monday. I had a phone call from Wendy yesterday. She called to tell me that if I was not successful in getting my dog certified as a care dog so she could be in my new home with me, that Phoebe could live with her. As she has already graciously provided me a room and a house key, this could become Phoebe's new home. I could spend as much time with her as I want and my dog would be with people who already love her. That call brought me to tears of gratitude for the amazing friends I have been blessed with. Wendy is one of many who have and continue to do so much to make this journey more bearable.

Sunday, April 9, 2017

Yesterday I was at my old job site to do photocopying for my presentation. I did not see everyone but those I did see reminded me of why and what I miss about my working career. So nice to see their faces, receive their hugs and share a smile, a laugh and the odd tear. I then spent the evening making sure I had it all together properly.

I felt good all day. I was going to have coffee with Sharon in the afternoon and ended up driving up towards Silver Star just enjoying the view then realized that I was actually supposed to be going to her house! I just thought, *oh well nice drive*, turned around and made my way there. Overall it was just a nice day.

Monday, April 10, 2017

I am so happy with how I have been feeling on this Aricept. Now that it has reached its correct levels it truly does allow me to function much better. It leaves me wondering what my new life purpose will be. Society is set up in such a way that a disability forces everything to stop instead of working to find ways that allow them to continue to contribute. Perhaps I need to learn that it's okay to slow down, that I don't have to keep pushing myself, yet I feel like I need to keep challenging my brain because my body is still so able. I started

63

Spanish lessons last fall, really wanted to keep going with it but could not afford the cost.

My brain does not shut off and I think about all those people in dementia units who are shuffled off to bed at 5:30-6 PM. Should they try to come out of their rooms they are quickly told to go back to bed. If they don't sleep all night, the caregivers want them medicated. It's so very wrong; we do harm this way.

Wednesday, April 12, 2017

It was nice to see my friends, Les and Terri, for a couple of days. We had some pretty big discussions about end of life issues and when we should recognize that it is kinder to stop intervening and allow people to go. We agreed Society goes too far with interventions these days.

I did my first presentation on living with dementia and feel it was well received. I have been asked to do another one in two weeks' time! I have also been asked to do a presentation to care aids at the college. I feel that if my having dementia can help one person understand better, then I have not let this disease destroy me. I felt like I had power over it even if only for a short time. I am grateful for the opportunity.

Friday, April 14, 2017

Today BMW was willing to help sell my little car when I am no longer able to drive so I can enjoy it until then. That's one more thing to put out of my mind.

The fog has lifted. It's fascinating to me just how much it impacts me from day to day. I don't think medications are the whole answer. I believe that by having a better understanding of how the symptoms affect cognitive skills, my day can be better managed and understood thus helping to minimize stress, anxiety, frustrations and in others, increased aggressive behaviors and agitation. I try to pay close attention to my mental state so I can have the best days possible. And that's why I believe that for people with dementia it is so important to allow them to wake and sleep as their body wants and needs. We may in fact be interfering with those precious REM and deep sleep times. Some may get them at 8 AM or 2 PM versus a person that gets them during a typical 10 PM to 7 AM sleep pattern. A lot of these types of things could and should be changed and the cost is minimal because it comes from willingness to change how and why care is given. I look forward to a long hike with my friend Naomi and am grateful that my night was such that my brain is going to allow it. Treasuring each good day being ever grateful.

Saturday, April 15, 2017

Dementia does not allow you to live but it doesn't allow you to die either. I am going out to an Easter brunch at (my niece) Tara's farm. The family is having an Easter egg hunt. I enjoy seeing everyone but at the same time am hesitant about it. I don't manage big groups very well, too much activity, noise and conversations all at once. I am determined to go and enjoy for the time I can manage.

Sunday, April 16, 2017

I was listening to a talk about dementia's effects on a person's vision. Although many with dementia have perfect vision, one's depth perception transmission is affected. I have perfect vision but my depth perception has always been very bad, lots of bumps, falls, and oopsies.

I brought this problem up in my talk last week and now I can better explain it. If you hold both your arms out to the side as far as you can; that is a young person's normal field of vision. Bring your arms half way to the front of you; that is what our field of vision narrows to as we age. Now move your arms parallel to the side of your face; that is the field of vision for someone with dementia. Then take a pair of binoculars and look through them as you walk; that is the area dementia patients focus on.

The ability to know how far down the chair is, where the floor is, where a light switch is, can't be judged correctly. I have known my depth perception was not good, what I did not know was it would be a sign of my dementia. Knowing allows me to pay attention and adjust my actions accordingly. I am extra cautious with stairs, parking and backing up my car. It explains my little crash into Kay's sister's car because I did not see it. Think about that when someone misses their mouth with their spoon, knocks over their glass of juice, struggles to get their arm in their sleeve or gets frightened by your approach.

The brain is such a fascinating thing and I am grateful that mine is allowing me the ability to share the effects this illness has on me. Hopefully what I share can help others understand and give them insight as they give care. Another of those silver linings.

Monday, April 17, 2017

I am in a rage at a system that fails daily, that refuses to think outside the box, a system that continually hides behind 'our policy and procedures,' allows statements of, "It's more complicated than you think." It sickens me. There are many ways to make things better, that are less wasteful of money and resources, but no one wants to actually acknowledge or listen to any ideas that are not part of a system which we already know does not work. It makes me angry when I hear that there is money to be spent to make a dementia unit better when in fact no amount of money will make that unit better, that unit does not work, cannot work. Do you know people in prisons are granted more outdoor space and outdoor time than those in the Dementia Unit? And I am tired of hearing the patients are exit-seeking! They are looking for a place to enjoy, they are looking to explore, they are looking for people to engage with!! I must fight hard to maintain independence for as long as I can so the system does not destroy what pieces and parts of me remain because I would be considered 'exit-seeking, or aggressive, or combative,' when all I really want is to be able to live with my disease in a way that is healthy and allows me to enjoy what's left for me.

Tuesday, April 18, 2017

My doctor's appointment went way longer than expected, but we had some of my team there and I am glad we are all on the same page.

We had big things to discuss, my health care directives, what I need for help currently, how medications are working, what the future holds, things the specialist will be looking at with me tomorrow. I am truly grateful for Dr. Cunningham, and the nurse practitioner he has on board is delightful!

The manager from my old work site called and said he was making up posters for my next presentation. He was sending it to the managers at the other sites, so hopefully I will be doing something there as well. May 5th is the next one.

I had to go get tires from my storage locker as I had made an appointment to have my tires swapped, no appointment on their books, weren't going to be able to have it ready till late. The guy takes the tires out of the bag and says, "One of these tires is no good so we can't put it on your car." Grrr. Then they can't decide if the type of tire can be run two and two. Nope I have to buy four new tires. This will cost me a minimum of $1000.00, plus taxes, fees.

I say, "Why was I not told when they took the tires off last fall that there was a problem with the tire?"

He says, "You should have been, another mistake. Sorry there's nothing we can do." This is a professional tire shop? I load the tires up, take them to storage then stop at another tire place.

He quotes me over $400.00 less for similar tires then says, "Well if you're not sure what you're doing car wise, why don't you just bring the car in and I'll rotate the winters you have on?"

I will save myself some money and, worst case scenario: buy new winter tires if I need them in the fall. Wow, thank you very much! I felt I was being taken advantage of at the first place. It's time to retreat to that quiet corner of the world where my brain can just relax and rest.

Wednesday, April 19, 2017

Yesterday I spent a few hours in quiet, without outside noise and external stimulation. That helped me have a better evening and hopefully helped set things up for a better day today.

I slept well last night but still woke with that painful head, the fog hovering, unsure if it is going to lift or envelope my brain. It's likely a leftover affect from trying to process too much yesterday. The more tired my brain gets the worse my memory becomes. It could become totally unmanageable if I did not understand what is happening and just stop and rest. It is quite frightening! For those further advanced I can understand why they become agitated and lash out. When I can no longer recognize it for myself I hope I always have someone around me who does.

Thursday, April 20, 2017

I had an appointment with my specialist, Dr. Pretorius, yesterday. He tested me and said the medicine is working, I am holding steady. All the things I do to help myself allows the medication to work as effectively as possible. He said all the walking I am doing helps tremendously. By monitoring what tires my brain, what situations are unmanageable, allowing proper rest times, I am giving myself the chance to stay at this level for a very long time. (Yippee!) No guarantees of course. I will smile about the good news.

He told me to keep doing presentations because too many people forget someone with dementia is still human, and that by giving people insight through my journey, it will give people a better understanding and will also help me. He made me cry a little because he said as a doctor, to have a patient who works so hard to find the good in devastation, to do so much to help herself is an inspiration to him. His sincerity was touching. Then my family doctor, Dr. Cunningham, called. He finished the paperwork to have Phoebe made into a service dog. Now I just need her papers from the vet, and a picture of her. Off the papers will go to the government, hopefully for approval. Another piece of good news.

Chapter Eight

Saturday, April 22, 2017

I am house sitting again. (Les and Cindy went to Jamaica for three weeks.).
Yesterday I forgot my medications. Thank goodness it was still early enough for me to take them when I finally noticed. Had a rest to settle my jumpy brain. I am thankful no one was here during the frustration part that left me screaming. I do believe I could have unintentionally lashed out because of how out of control everything felt.

I was able to enjoy a lovely dinner with my friend June. The evening was spent sitting quietly visiting.

Late last night, as I was lying in bed reading, I received a message from another friend telling me a friend of hers who spent years working in a Dementia Unit was just diagnosed with dementia and could I connect with her. She was already reading some if my writings and felt things were ringing very true for her as well. I added her to my page. We had a lengthy chat via Facebook. She is only 61, her diagnosis is very new, she has many appointments, a new routine and her doctor has already pulled her driver's license. My heart broke for her and I hope we can be a great support to each other. Her biggest fear, just like mine, was ending up in a facility. For us who know so much, the dread is all too real.

Sunday, April 23, 2017

Fatigued again. Yesterday evening I was doing my Sudoku puzzle book and getting frustrated. I kept writing numbers, but my brain kept telling me it wanted a different number. If I thought I was writing a four for example, I was actually writing a five. Hopefully today will be enjoyable regardless.

My step-children came to visit, Natasha and Jacob with their daughter Emily, and Brenden with his wife Erika. Brent and Kay came to visit as well. We sat out on the patio enjoying the pleasant weather. Erika just glowed and eventually we found out why. She and Brenden are expecting twins! I was so happy for them; so were their aunt and uncle.

Tuesday, April 25, 2017

Today is my 58th birthday. I look back at the last year and am amazed I am still standing. Even though it is a day to celebrate it comes with a sadness that sits deep inside. But I also have to celebrate that I am still here and I have been victorious thus far. I can see, in the not so distant future, dinner engagements will have to be turned into breakfast or lunch engagements. Although it has taken me three days to put together a cake, I am determined to finish it today and hope I didn't miss any important steps or ingredients.

Wednesday, April 26, 2017

I slept and rested most of the day yesterday. By late afternoon I was able to finish my cake although it did not turn out quite as good as I had hoped. A lovely wiener roast at Brent and Kay's, small, manageable for me, and being rested really helped.

This morning I am going to start looking after the flowers at the Flower Spot Plant Nursery a few hours at a time. It will only be for a couple months but will keep me looking forward to something. On good days I feel like I could manage for a long time; on bad ones I feel like it is all unraveling so fast that I can't catch my breath.

Saturday, April 29, 2017

Helping at the nursery a few hours a day is great because it's full of life, things growing, blossoming. It is good for me in many ways, a different focus even if just for a short time each day. It is always tiring, so monitoring myself, not over-tiring my brain, very important if I want to do this little piece of normal.

Monday, May 1, 2017

The last two days have been good to me, the fog has lifted again and I have been feeling well. It's a battle not to slip into convincing myself that I am better because it is so desperately what I want. With the medication working so well, I am ready for my own place again. It's been wonderful to have this safe haven here with Brent and Kay. It has afforded me the ability to figure out how to live with this disease and I know I am ready to begin building a new and totally different life and manage it for as long as I can.

Tuesday, May 2, 2017

Yesterday started out so good, but in the afternoon I ended up in the ER with an apparent heart attack! So more new medications, more setbacks – ugh. They will do tests today. There is so much information to go over with the doctors. They have been great as have all the staff, all shocked that I have dementia because I am young, many openly admitting they know very little about it. One doctor who queried the level of resuscitation I would allow was quite interested in understanding the reasons for my choices. In the end, she said she didn't blame me for making the choices I have. So, to go from her being shocked to her understanding and respecting was uplifting in a strange way. The heart doctor was very kind, very compassionate, said there is such irony in the situation. I am just hoping this does not cause another slip on the Dementia Trail. On we go to a revised plan.

Wednesday, May 3, 2017

I'm sitting in my 6th floor room in Vernon Jubilee Hospital awaiting more tests. They may not be able to do much as the root cause is my cerebra-vascular disease and it limits them. The best I can do is get new medicines to keep the blood flowing as much as possible. It's very hard on my heart as well as my brain when these already tiny vessels constrict further. I am sad that I have to cancel my presentation on Friday and reschedule it for another time. I will post when I have rescheduled.

It's funny: normally I am not the best patient but this time it has forced me to take some reflection time. The staff have been good about taking their time to explain and re-explain what's happening. I guess at the end of the day I will know the important bits and pieces and the rest doesn't matter. I will, of course, have new medications when I am released. They are not as knowledgeable about dementia as they would like to be, they are amazed that it's happening to people so young, their interest tells me we need to do so much more about educating people. I spoke to Jo yesterday. We talked about the difficulties some have in acknowledging our illness and how people struggle to understand how we can be so accepting. Neither of us wishes to waste what precious time and energy we have while we are still high functioning, to anger, bitterness and sadness. We want to put memories in the files of our brain so maybe later those things will bring us pieces of happiness.

Tina Rowe wrote to Christine on May 3, 2017

I really enjoyed seeing you today; I know you were tired. I love that no matter how bad things are you find the positive! You are stubborn when it comes to asking for help! Your independent nature is probably what gets you through. You say you never NEED anything but you do! Your next step is accepting and asking for help when you need it. We are your friends and family and if we can't help in some way, we also feel a sense of loss. We are all here for you because we love you so let us coddle you when we can; it helps us as much as you!

Christine's answer May 4, 2017

Wow, my dear friend Tina Rowe, your visit yesterday was so good for me, so appreciated. Thank you for all your kindness. I read your words and your sincerity struck such a chord in me. I have been thinking of all you have said and you are quite right, I don't ask for help. I guess that comes from having to learn to go it alone after my husband died. When we have been independent and self-sufficient it becomes difficult to admit we can no longer manage on our own. I also try to always be respectful of the fact that others have busy lives and just because I am alone it does not mean I have a right to expect them to help me. I hope if people think I need something they will ask or just do.

I honestly don't have any idea what my needs might be. When I sit and think what do I need? All that comes to mind is nothing, I don't really need anything. I wish I knew how to do this part better so it would be easier for my friends. Just know that whatever you do is appreciated and whatever you feel I may need is welcomed. Things have changed so much for me in such a relatively short period of time, figuring out my needs seems to have become a real challenge. I think that what I need is love from family and friends.

Your lovely gift inspired my doctor to give the nurses permission to finally allow me a much needed and much enjoyed shower: so, for the shampoo, lovely soap, deodorant, tooth paste, socks, and other goodies, thanks. You helped make this girl feel so much better. Hugs to you!

Friday, May 5, 2017

Yesterday was the pivotal day for me. Things were taking a turn for the better; decisions were being made, a coming-back day.

Today was not as good. Unsure of where I was several times; had to lie down and go through my check list, too much stimulation and too much to process. Nurses and doctors took extra time to go over things with me and let me go back to my room to process the information then come back to go over it all again. They sat with me and wrote down my questions so that when the specialist came I wouldn't forget. He was so kind and took the time to really make sure I understood why one procedure would be done versus another.

Thank goodness the chest pain is under control, medications doing their job. I will have a CT Angiogram Monday and then will be sprung. I was so grateful to have Dr. Cunningham arrive yesterday (even though he doesn't do hospital rounds anymore) and bring along with him two great specialists to ensure the best outcome I can have. The specialist said that if they need to fix something beyond the use of medications, unless it could be done without too much risk I should likely choose not to do it and enjoy my window of good days before the dementia robs me of that. Quality not quantity. Feeling tired, but on the mend and oh so very humbled and grateful for all the amazing people who I have in my life professionally and personally.

Another TIA likely happened during the night contributing to my issues, including chest pain, pain between shoulder blades, legs tingling, sweats, fast pulse, high BP. They decided to increase the medications to their original level for the time being.

Sunday, May 7, 2017

I spent a very quiet day yesterday thinking about all the people I know who are facing serious health issues. Dementia is a terminal illness but a long drawn out one, there is no option to stop treatments when I've had enough, yet it's okay, I still get this window of time that I can be fairly high functioning. When I spring out of here I will be doing and enjoying as much as possible, there will be no such thing as, "Do you think you should slow down?" Because the answer will be NO and if I end up with a heart or stroke issue that takes me out. LET IT. It will mean I am lucky. I will have enjoyed that window instead of wasting it sitting scared because something might happen.

Someone said to me that perhaps I shouldn't go to Kamloops when I get out but stay home and rest instead. I just smiled. I did cancel my work at the garden center and my upcoming trip to Niagara Falls and instead will spend quality time with my sister and my family and I will go to Kamloops because, as the specialist said, "Our goal is to help you enjoy the window before your dementia closes it."

Monday, May 8, 2017

I had an interesting event take place; some people working here had my chart in their hand and stated, "She comes to us from community." We in health care are all familiar with that phrase. It means I am now flagged because I have dementia; they are trying to make sure I don't fall between the cracks. I understand but it seems surreal that one month you are working in the system the next month the system is working on you.

Tuesday, May 16, 2017

My doctors have done a good job of getting the right mix of medications, been out of hospital one week today, have not had the dreadful Dementia Fog. The other symptoms persist but are more manageable. My sleep is also much improved, so with improved blood flow comes better days. I am hopeful for a good number of months and will strive for a good five or six years. Yup, forever being positive.

I have signed up for a dementia course that starts in July; if it can help me in this journey in any way then I want to take it. It is out of the Tasmania University Dementia Research and Education department and will be a nine-week course. I am looking forward to it. I spent the last week in Kamloops very quietly recuperating and resting and am feeling stronger every day. I am now back home in Vernon.

Wednesday, May 17, 2017

When my friend Terri visited me last week, we were out for a couple of hours doing some things she needed to do and I realized that piece of me that used to love hunting for great little shopping spots and places to take my friends is locked away somewhere deep inside that filing cabinet. I have a necklace that hangs in my car now that says, "All who wander are not lost." Terri thought it was perfect. It reminds me not to panic; I am on an adventure.

Thursday, May 18, 2017

Talking with my sister-in-law Kay about the difference between now and when I went into the hospital. She said I was living in a very bewildered state. The fog is not so thick; I am less bewildered. My friend Barb told me I really have no concept of time anymore.

Friday, May 19, 2017

I talked to another lady last night about her struggles with her dementia and being on her own. Afterward I wondered if it really would be any better if we weren't on our own or would we be feeling like we were a burden, that it wasn't fair to a partner? I for sure wish my husband was here by my side through this but most of the time I am grateful that he doesn't have to watch it.

Sunday, May 21, 2017

I was supposed to go house sitting for a few days; I finally had to say no. When there are curve balls thrown at me it knocks my whole being off. Yesterday Brent and Kay were having a big family reunion; I visited early and very briefly. I ended up fatigued from poor sleep thus causing more problems like forgetting my dinner pills and departing early because of too much noise and commotion. Their understanding and support on bad days is always so appreciated. I cried driving home; it was a sad day. Today my headache is back; it hasn't been there since I came out of the hospital.

Tuesday, May 23, 2017

Out for a drive visiting different small communities: I was astounded at how many of those places I remembered staying in but could not remember why, when or who I was with.

I was having coffee with a friend, looking at her plants, used to know without hesitation their names. I could picture the plants in my mind but could not retrieve the names. Other days I can look at a plant and instantly remember its name. The hard part is that I don't get to decide what I can manage and what I can't on any given day. I do know that since the blood flow has been improved, since my heart is not working so hard, it has helped me immensely.

Thursday, May 25, 2017

My doctors want me to get back to walking as much as I feel I can manage: physiotherapy and Pilates every week, building up to four times a week by July, so important for blood flow. Happy to have the green light to continue to drive for now; this causes me great excitement but I have to listen when the brain fog says 'not today.' I struggle to remember to take my medications but I'm learning how to set reminders on my phone. I lost my pajamas yesterday, have spent hours trying to find them to no avail.

Sunday, May 28, 2017

SPRUCE GROVE, AB: Yesterday I left for the first road trip I have been able to attempt for a long time, June in tow. I could not attempt this without someone with me. I was feeling apprehensive before we left but also excited at the thought of enjoying that sense of freedom I adore so much. We left Kelowna to first visit friends, Les and Terri, in Valemount. It was a beautiful day, top down, warm sunshine; I had a great sleep the night before, taking our time, sightseeing along the way, Mad River, Avola and a world-famous burger, Little Hell's Gate. Being in Valemount again opened the floodgates of memories where I was happy and content. It felt good to have these resurface.

Today we drove to Edmonton stopping along the way. I was sad to see a forest fire but Mount Robson was spectacular as always in the early morning sun. On to Jasper which is already busy, a pretty drive to Hinton where we stopped to stretch then on to Edson for lunch. Into Edmonton to visit and have a lovely dinner with Sharon who we worked with in Kelowna. After, I went for a nice walk then enjoyed the evening visiting. Much to be thankful for.

Wednesday, May 31, 2017

I finished the rest of the journey to Gronlid, Saskatchewan. I did get a little panicky driving the last couple hours on my own, after I dropped June off in Saskatoon. I kept reminding myself that I had my GPS. I was able to remain calm but my confidence in my ability to navigate on my own has sure changed. I don't think I will venture into areas that I am unfamiliar with on my own any longer.

I came to see my niece Nichole's children, Lexy, Tyson and Brayden at their dad's place. My visit here has been fabulous; spending time with the kids has done my heart good. This has been a great place of healing for them. I have had full but not exhaustive days, no wearing myself out.

Nichole has been a steady person in my life since the day she was born and over the years I have helped her through many difficult times, including having her and her two children Alexis and Tyson live with me while she was pregnant with Brayden so she could go to school to provide a better life for herself.

After she left things went well for a number of years. I always helped whenever it was needed and spent as much time as possible with all of them. However, Nichole never recovered from the loss of Max, a friend who helped provide her with a type of stability no one else was able to give her. Her life with her partner Danny was tumultuous; although they love each other immensely they were not good for each other. Nichole's subsequent battles with different drugs soon began to unravel things for her and her children.

I tried to help but her addictions were too strong. Eventually I had to step back, in part to try and force her to get the help she needed and also because, as my health declined, I was no longer able to provide the assistance required. The three kids ended up in Saskatchewan with their dad and, when I travelled to see them, my niece Alexis was upset with me because she thought I was just mad at her mom and that's why I wasn't helping. Little did she know I still sent messages to encourage Nichole to get help and to know she is loved. I shared all of those texts with Alexis, which helped her to understand what was really transpiring with her mom. I miss the children dearly and wish I was closer and hope to manage another trip to see them.

Saturday, June 3, 2017

I did fairly well on this journey not to overtire my brain until yesterday. I think all the emotions of the week, saying goodbye which was so difficult then driving longer than I should have because June did not want another stop-over, was too much. I will not be pushing; I will be taking it slowly, enjoying the day. I will make it home sometime tomorrow. I have a headache but overall still doing and feeling better than I have for a long while. When I can't do simple things like pump gas and talk to someone at the same time, can't drive in the city and have a conversation at the same time, can't follow directions or figure the directions out, I am acutely aware of how things have changed.

Chapter Nine

Wednesday, June 7, 2017

I can't explain to anyone how truly grateful I am to all the doctors who worked so hard so they could give me this window. I was not thinking I could ever feel as good as I do right now. If this window lasts ten days or five years, I will always be thankful. I was talking to my sister-in-law yesterday and she is astounded by the difference. I am spending time paying attention to paperwork, finances, all the things I thought I was managing better than I was. I am walking again, still not as much as before but I will get there. I keep myself in check because I must not overdo anything, although it sure makes me want to. I am off to Penticton for the day and enjoying the sunshine.

Saturday, June 10, 2017

I sleep in! I am getting 6 to 7 hours sleep versus, 2 to 5, so important for my brain. An ankle that was fractured well over a year ago is finally healed, apparently it was not getting the correct blood flow. I still have challenges and struggles, but am much better able to deal with them, able to make better decisions. I still doubt myself sometimes but I am able to enjoy life as it should be enjoyed. I am very humbled by what this disease is teaching me.

Monday, June 12, 2017

Still wondering how much the change of barometric pressure affects the Dementia Brain. I shall be monitoring this in the future because the last couple of days the high and low air pressure systems having been changing a lot and sometimes quite quickly.

I am getting ready for my next little road trip, this one will be my first on my own in a very long time – yikes, a little nervous. I packed a picnic lunch so I can just relax, take my time and enjoy the journey. Excited to see my family. My brother is home from Manitoba so will get a chance to visit with him.

Thinking a lot about my husband today. I know he watches over me and on my hardest days I can hear him whisper, "It's okay Chrissy, you can do this." I am looking for and finding the diamond in the day.

Wednesday, June 14, 2017

HOSMER BC: I did enjoy my trip over here but was surprised at how many blank spots I have of where I was. I have travelled this road many times before. However, there were things and places that triggered memories: like a small motel where I stayed one very cold winter's night coming from or going to a visit with my parents. Going through an area close to my hometown I stopped for a work zone. A young man working on the road crew looked exactly like my very dear friend who passed away around the time my husband did. I am sure it was his son. Memories flooded back from years ago.

Old memories come quite well; it's the memories from the last five to ten years that seem to have left me. If I have blank spots, at least the memories that are there are ones I am happy to carry and cherish.

Sunday, June 17, 2017

Two days ago, I enjoyed a wonderful evening visiting with my brother, sister, nieces and nephews, lots of laughs as always.

Yesterday started a relaxing road trip with my sister, loads of fun, nothing stressful, no pressure. We are doing a trip our brother mapped out for us in place of the trip to Niagara Falls that twice had to be cancelled due to my health.

We started exploring in Orofino, Idaho, amazing bakery, super friendly people. Then on to Lewiston, so much bigger than I expected, beautiful drive, breath taking views, and the stunning farms on the plateau were totally unexpected. On to Moscow, Idaho, enjoyed an open market, enjoyed exploring the town, busy place, again so much more than expected. The sun was shining, the scenery beautiful, lots of laughter, lots if shared memories. On to Coeur d'Alene and from there to Sand Point. I really enjoyed the healing garden we found, such a peaceful place, reminisced about our childhood trips here. Relaxed for the evening, the adventure continues tomorrow.

Friday, June 23, 2017

My little Phoebe is getting old, sleeping a lot, short walks only, fell down again today. Her little leg popped out of place again, I had to carry her until it went back in, feeling sad.

Saturday, June 24, 2017

Today I will try to write and have it actually BE here. Funny, did I actually write my blog the other day and it disappeared or did I write it in my mind but not on the computer? I had a bad spell the other night, my heart was racing then it got stuck and was just vibrating. I thought I was going to have to go back to hospital but eventually it settled down. It did leave me tired yesterday so I had a pretty quiet day.

Tuesday, June 27, 2017

Sunday, I had surprise visitors come into town for the night; I recently stayed overnight with them on my way to Saskatchewan. Then yesterday, after my physio/Pilates hour, I was able to re-connect for lunch. I was early so I decided to stroll through the mall, not something I have been able to do with any ease for a long time. Walking past the restaurant where I was to meet my friends, someone banged on the window. It was a group of my former co-workers so I went in. It was so good to see them. How I miss the camaraderie and friendships from work; it was nice to catch up. My out of town friends joined us. By the end of the meal the background noise was becoming a challenge so my visitor and I headed off.

Yesterday was so enjoyable, yes, I did miss parts of the conversations, yes, my brain had trouble switching from one person to the other, but I managed, I enjoyed, I was able to engage. The rest of the day was spent quietly, I realized that it had been enough stimulation for me. But oh it felt so good.

I am going to Penticton with a friend of mine to help run an RV Park. I can do bookings and greet customers as it works for me. I am excited for this new lease on life; it will mean coming back and forth for my doctor appointments but I will eventually return here on a permanent basis. I am not leaving until mid-September. It feels good to be making some plans instead of fighting with everything I have in me to make it through the day. This move will allow me to socialize as much as I feel I am able from day to day, it will mean less chance of being isolated. I am truly grateful to have a friend that can help me to maintain a life again.

Friday, June 30, 2017

I have moved from Kay and Brent's to their next-door neighbor's house to look after their dog while they take a camper trip across Canada for two months.

Tuesday, July 4, 2017

About two days ago I realized I have lost my sense of taste unless it's very spicy, sour or super sweet.

I think about all those who have been helping me navigate these waters; they are just as important to me sharing my good moments with as they have been sharing the difficult ones.

Saturday, July 8, 2017

Friends now tell me it used to be frightening watching me trying to get through my days. One described it as like I had the door closed then after a couple of very scary challenging years had a window open. I'm thankful for the window but terrified of the day it shuts.

My new adventure in Penticton will give me a sense of purpose, a direction, and I will embrace it for as long as I can. It will move me a couple hours from where I am now but to an area that has always been near and dear to me. I will be steps away from Okanagan Lake and all who know me know of my love of water. My life will be shared with a very dear friend so I won't be totally on my own. I have many things to be thankful for.

Tuesday, July 11, 2017

Yesterday I was exhausted, confused, trying to remember where I was, sleep disturbed. At one point just saying to myself no, no, no! It is terrifying to have this slip.

Thursday, July 13, 2017

Walking, resting, working on things that are pleasurable, working on things that bring happiness, doing lots of stretching. Missed and mixed up appointments. I used to get so upset at myself about those things because I was always so punctual. Now I laugh at it all except forgetting medications; that's something that I really have to be diligent about. By the time I move I will have a lot of things that have been neglected done, updated and checked off my list.

Friday, July 14, 2017

Yesterday was not so great; I will monitor myself closely this weekend and see the doctor on Monday if there is no improvement. I am sure it is triggered by a few different factors, the long heat wave we've been having, smoke from all the forest fires and stress. I have dealt with the stress. I am trying to be very careful in the heat but I can't do anything about the smoke except stay inside. I have the ability to have as much quiet time as I need to look after myself so I will take it.

Saturday, July 15, 2017

Today is a much better day for me, head is clear again, pain is gone, sleep returned to somewhat normal. Feeling like I have staved off the beast for another spell. My new mission: to keep chasing the beast away. However, Kay just popped by with the gentle reminder to not overdo it, slow down. Floors washed, vacuuming done, bathroom cleaned, so enough for today. I had a lovely walk at 6 AM; the air was fresh and relatively cool. Between 5 and 7 AM is the best time with this intense heat.

Balance, balance, balance, life is all about balance. Unfortunately, my generation grew up in a time when we were pushed to do more, work, look after home and family and give, give, give OF ourselves without any time left to give TO ourselves. Then one day my body and mind said, "Okay, that's it." If we are lucky, we are given the chance to make changes that allow us to continue with life albeit in a different fashion and style than maybe we thought we should have.

I find I have come to a place where I no longer have the time or patience for people who are ungrateful or negative all the time; it drains my wellbeing. I am still kind, caring and compassionate, but I am not as tolerant.

Monday, July 24, 2017

I am not liking all the things forgotten over the last little bit; where are my blue cooler, misplaced car keys, forgotten appointments? I have to find my cooler, I will need it for moving, I don't want to have to buy another one. I am feeling the frustration of having everything scattered. Sometimes and in some ways having my illness allows others to take advantage. I'm trying to put things back into order, rebuild, take back control. Today I am mad at the beast. I will go to my storage locker and look for a few things I cannot seem to find.

Tuesday, July 25, 2017

There are people out there who prey on people who are vulnerable. I had turned to a company that was supposed to be providing me with help organizing my finances because I was struggling to remember and I didn't want to burden friends and family with things that I feel I should do myself. It wasn't until months later, when I came out of the hospital this last time and had some better brain days that I realized something did not seem right. After weeks of trying to sort through and figure it all out I realized I had been scammed. It came at a huge financial cost to me…not an easy thing to admit to or talk about but I was taken advantage of.

I am recovering, but it is humiliating to think I allowed this to happen, that I couldn't see it. Thankfully I figured out what was going on before it cost me anymore than it did. Not everyone who says they are trying to help truly is. I am even more grateful to my doctors for giving me this window that has allowed me enough clarity to catch this and get it ended. Yesterday was my day to feel ripped off, not only by a bad company, but by an illness that some days robs me of too much. Today is a better day.

I am happy to say that the company in question is being fully investigated and unable to do business at the moment. Their license has been pulled. I will recover at least a portion…I can say it's actually good things happened as they did or I would maybe not have known for some time to come…it has taken me weeks and weeks trying to get this all dealt with but am hoping soon it will be behind me, I am one of the fortunate ones…apparently this kind of stuff happens all the time.

It is time to let the authorities do what they must, have faith that what is mine will be returned, and in the meantime focus on all the good things. I do realize that sometimes it is easy for one thing to compound another and the smallest thing becomes the tipping point and shows you there is something bigger you must deal with.

Thursday, July 27, 2017

So I have been taking a dementia course through the Tasmania University…find it fascinating…the brain…amazed at my knowledge level but still so much to learn…trying to help myself…still my passion…not working it anymore…living it instead…crazy how life goes…lessons each and every day…some good some not so good, but life is about learning…feeling happy with the new chapter I am embarking on…going to have a life again…been too long without one…no matter for how long…it's a life…feeling excited, been watching everyone else's life evolving for a few years while mine was disappearing, so grateful to have this window to have my own life again. So very grateful.

Sunday, July 30, 2017

I forgot pills a couple times this last week and have been struggling with this sinus issue since coming out of the hospital. It's causing headaches…ugh. Waiting and waiting for special approval needed for the medication the doctor prescribed to clear it up. I'm also waiting for special approval for my Aricept; I only have enough for five more days. I don't know why the doctor has to keep reapplying for the special approval; I hate thinking I could end up not having it for a spell.

Because it is a special authority required medication the drug store won't give out any to fill the gap. Frustrating beyond words, calls to the doctor's office every couple of days, calls and going to the drug store constantly trying to get this stuff done so I can have my prescription. I'm hoping by tomorrow for sure.

Otherwise I'm feeling so at ease about my upcoming move…like it's just supposed to be that way, no worries, fears or hesitations about it. I'll miss my friends but I don't see them as often as I once did. They have responsibilities to their partners which must and should come first. And I have changed. So, it's good to be moving in some direction, even if not the expected one, a new chapter is before me, my book of life is large, it's been full, it's been happy, sad, hard, challenging, exciting, devastating, but I have had so much to be thankful for and I am sure that this new chapter will again lend itself to much.

Chapter Ten

The plan to go to Penticton was hatched when my friend Markus and I realized we could likely help each other if we found a job doing something we would both enjoy. This became a real possibility during the summer and fall of 2016 when we earnestly starting looking at the possibilities. We decided an RV park would be manageable for us both as Markus had once owned one. We were searching various job sites on the internet when the opportunity in Penticton popped up. We applied and went through the process of interviews with the couple who owned the business.

Eventually we were told we were overqualified for the position and that they felt that it would not be enough for us. They then chose the second in line for the job. These people were scheduled to start in March, 2017, but at the end of February, we were told, they backed out due to health issues. The owners wanted to know if we were still interested and after much discussion we decided yes, but we could not start until mid-September due to other commitments. We then went back and forth a couple of times, meeting mostly with the wife, Sue, going over policies and procedures.

In late August, after getting verbal permission from her, we took a few things down to store prior to our full move and had another talk with both owners. That time the husband's real personality came through and we decided not to go forward with the job.

Tuesday, August 1, 2017, email sent to owners of the Trailer Park:

Dear Sue,

I just wanted to touch base. I have been going over our visit yesterday because I was quite shocked by Dave's handling of things. Unfortunately, the tires were a miscommunication between Markus and myself so I apologize for that. (This is not quite the truth but I was trying to be diplomatic.) However, I do believe their arrival could have been handled differently. We have been trying to stay in touch, showing our commitment to come on board and taking the position of managers very seriously by coming to spend some time on site to see how things are being done. We wanted to get to know you, the property and the business a little to allow for an easier transition come September.

To hear that I could have gotten a storage unit for my possessions was truly insulting. If I had known it would create a hardship, we would not have even thought of bringing anything. We did not ever consider bringing things ahead of our arrival as a way to take advantage only as a way to help with the transition. I am in hopes that in the future we will have a better line of communication if something needs to be discussed. We hope this is not going to dampen what could be a long working relationship for all of us as we have always stated we are committed to a long-term arrangement.

Sincerely, Christine.

Wednesday, August 2, 2017, email written after a phone call to Christine from Dave wherein he laid down the law:

Sue,

First off, let me again tell you how sorry I am for the situation you are facing with your father (he was dying). It is always difficult no matter how well we think we are prepared and we truly feel for you.

We are writing to give our 30 days' notice to dissolve the contract which was to begin on September 16, 2017. Unfortunately, it has become apparent that our two styles of doing business are not going to be as cohesive as we had hoped and feel it is best to stop now. Further to our conversation, Dave, you made it abundantly clear that we would not meet your standards and that you have many red flags.

This is not a good way to start a working relationship. You explained that there would be many 'heated' conversations and that we should expect to be reprimanded. In our business lives, we believe respectful communication, explaining and showing what is required carries far more value than yelling at people and using heated discussions as a way to get things accomplished. We understood you wanted us to be able to manage but, clearly, your ideas of how employees/managers should be treated are not in line with ours.

We firmly believe in working extremely hard and giving our very best but also expect to be treated with a level of respect which we do not feel would be forthcoming. We fully understand the work involved in running a business and had expected to manage it in accordance with your policies. This was not a job we 'needed,' it was something we enjoy and were fully capable of managing. It was not about you doing us a 'favor' or us doing you a 'favor.' It was something that could have been good for both parties which is how a working relationship should be.

Being told it will always be about you and your business and never about us was surprising. We had believed that perhaps all of the reviews from customers we read were a little misguided but in light of recent events we now believe the treatment the guests were speaking of is clearly also the way in which employees or managers would be treated and in our view is absolutely unacceptable. We regret having to do this at such a time for you Sue, but believe it is better to do it now than have the upheaval of us coming and then being told in a month to leave.

Please let me know a convenient time for me to retrieve the items we have there. We are happy to do it whenever it is best for you given the situation at hand.

Sincerely, Markus and Christine.

Saturday, August 5, 2017

I haven't written for a bit, the last few weeks have been challenging, and I found myself struggling on many levels. I was wondering if I wanted to write anymore. My self-confidence is eroded so I have been lying low, going deep within, slowly emerging. I know that at the end of the day we are fortunate we did not get to Penticton, have things go sideways and have to move again.

Time for a new plan but I am not even trying to figure it out right now; I am just putting things out to God and asking for help, for direction, for clarity and having faith that I will end up where I am meant to be. I know that I really need to have a home of my own again. I have been so blessed to have people give me a safe haven when I was not well enough to be on my own.

Yesterday I sat with Kara, the Integrated Care Coordinator with Interior Health, who helped me go through all the things that are important for me at this time and to ensure that as I need help in the future, they are already preparing the plan.

She made me realize that I am struggling to make decisions because of not trusting my brain and my abilities any longer. It is important for me to continue to make decisions. If I mess up, oh well, I am trying and I am doing the best I can. People can make bad decisions even without being faced with such a challenging illness. I have to remember, that even if I mess things up, they can be fixed.

A couple of possibilities have come to me and I am letting them bounce around. I am not going to force it; I am going to trust in it being shown to me. I am giving in, letting go, but not giving up on having the best life I can for as long as I can.

I have just sat down and said, "Okay God, you have to stop now. I know you never give us more than we can handle, but I feel you're tipping the scale too far, I'm too close to falling off the edge. It's time for you to give me a reprieve and send some good things my way." Still standing!

Sunday, August 6, 2017

Even though I have been questioning whether I should keep doing this, after writing yesterday, I can't tell you how much good it did to just admit to all who know me that I'm not always okay. I have an amazing group of friends and family who are so very good to me, I am so blessed and grateful to them, but they cannot be there always and I cannot and will not overburden them just because I am alone. I strategize with myself; I bargain with myself; I constantly have mental conversations with myself to help get through another day. We culturally have been taught to plan for the future, we aren't taught what to do when there is no future. In the end, all I can do is make a decision based on how I feel today at this moment. Today has more clarity, less emotion, more realism, more practicality. I am writing about this because it helps me work through it and perhaps it will help someone out there understand what the emotional and mental tolls are, not just the physical and neurological challenges.

Monday, August 7, 2017

All the smoke in the air from the fires is causing my vessels to become inflamed, the inflammation is then causing a decrease in blood flow, lack of blood flow, lack of oxygen to the brain. I am so weak I feel like I am going to collapse, so the only way to help myself is to go to bed and let my body relax and not struggle to stay upright. My heart goes out to all those guys fighting those fires. I can't imagine how difficult it is for them and the stress it puts their bodies under.

I have some big choices coming up within the next two weeks and I am trying to just let God show me which decision I should be making. I want to move by October 1st and I am applying for my dog to be licensed as a service dog. If she cannot be, then I am faced with the heartache of having to give her up. However, I am equally aware of how important it is for me to have my own place for as long as my health will allow. I have a couple of options in housing but none allow me to keep my dog without a license. I'm not sure how long the process will take and whether, at her age, she can manage all the testing required; there is a list of 40 things she must be able to complete with ease. I'm leaving it in God's hands; too difficult for me to make the decision. I need a stretch of positive things to happen. My body is tired, my soul is tired, my mind is tired.

Wednesday, August 9, 2017

This last setback has been the first time I have said to myself okay, I'm done, I've had enough, I can't manage anymore. Then yesterday, through the kindness of others, my worries were lessened by help to find a home for myself and my dog. I now have a place to go to as of September 1st. I am not sure how apartment living will work for me, but I am sure I will be happy because I will have my little Phoebe with me. I am grateful to all those who helped in my search, I am grateful to all those who have said they will be there to help with the move, it takes a huge stress off me to know I will have the help I need.

Today another friend stepped up and took me to Penticton to retrieve the things that needed to come back and I am so very grateful for her help and support. I am exhausted emotionally and mentally but again feeling like I can and will continue to fight a good fight for as long as I can so I can continue to see and enjoy my people.

Saturday, August 12, 2017

I have an O2 concentrator for now to help with getting enough oxygen to my brain. An RN at Gateby donated it to me. Dr. Cunningham does not want me to end up with another permanent step down. He said my cardio-vascular system is working too hard right now and we need to help it until the air quality etc. here improves. I slept last night, I even slept in this morning, my heart was not stopping multiple times through the night, my brain was not oxygen deprived. I'm sure, over the next few days, I will continue to see improvement in my cognitive being.

Sunday, August 13, 2017

Yesterday was much better until late afternoon, then fatigue. I could not carry on a conversation, dizzy, weak…hum. Very likely another TIA. The O2 concentrator is doing its job though so feel clearer headed this morning. It will be a quiet day again. Some days I feel like a slug moving in slow motion.

Maybe this rain will clear the air and my heart won't be overtaxed. I signed up to be part of an online study group with the Mayo Clinic so will hopefully help someone else down the road.

Wednesday, August 16, 2017

I hate my specialist seeing me like this. It's so raw and real and truly not something that feels good to have others witness. Still, I always end up feeling better after visiting him. He told me he stood on the stairs for a few moments watching me and he could see another event had happened; he could see it on my face and he could see the physical exhaustion.

After discussing all that has happened lately, he said I am perfectly right to feel all the things I am feeling and that I acknowledge them is very healthy. He doesn't know of anyone who fights harder than I do to try to help myself and do everything I can for my wellbeing.

He would not do testing today because it would be unfair, my brain and body are too fatigued to give true results which could trigger all kinds of things: like my ability to drive taken away. No testing now until late October, giving me a chance to get moved, settled and recouped from this last event. Dr. Cunningham called and wants to see me again Friday.

Friday, August 18, 2017

Today has been another day of realizations. Dr. Cunningham said I am too hard on myself; I have to realize that because I do all the things I do to stay as well as I can and help myself as much as I can, I am still functioning well. He said that if I wasn't doing all of those things, I would be having TIAs every 5 to 7 days and likely some larger strokes.

They are going to do another scan, a CT not an MRI as he does not want me to have to pay for another MRI. Next, I will be getting a life line, likely by the end of September, and I have come to the conclusion along with my doctors that I will be giving up my car, likely by the end of October, not my license just yet, but my car. I will hold my license so if I really wanted to go somewhere, I could rent a car. Giving up driving in baby steps; again, I am a realist. I will enjoy my little car until then. Lots to absorb, truly an unbelievable few weeks.

Saturday, August 19, 2017

So, my sister-in-law asked me this morning how I feel. I said my first thought when I woke up was that I was in an emotional thunderstorm. On one side so excited and grateful for all the hard work Warren and Cara are doing to renovate my apartment ready for the first of September. At the same time, I am overcome with a deep sadness at the thought of not having my car and not driving. I do feel it is better to do it this way as it allows me time to adjust. I won't apologize for being all over the map emotionally; I am going out to buy a toaster for my new home.

Sunday, August 20, 2017

The second day of actually sleeping for more than twenty minutes at a time really helped me regain strength. I was able to get up this morning and actually think about the upcoming week and all that I need to accomplish in preparation for the move. My time house sitting for the neighbors will be up at the end of the month. I will continue to do house sitting even after I move, just not on a full-time basis. Once I am settled in my new place, I can work on enjoying life again, finding ways to fill my days, maybe taking a course if I can afford it.

I have to finish my university course on dementia; it's so very important. I am feeling pretty proud that I got 100% on everything so far. I understand it in ways that are unexplainable except to say that it all makes sense to me, the pathology of it all. I have a clear picture of what is happening inside my brain, I understand and know when I am having another TIA, I am not always able to do the things I should during those times because the brain is not functioning properly, but I understand it.

I know that as the disease progresses my abilities will decrease but by understanding and listening to what my body is telling me I hope to continue to help myself stay upright and independent for a good long time. I have to remember to get a plastic sleeve to put my DNR into and have it on my fridge door…priorities how they shift and change…feeling better today, feeling like today will bring about some laughter and smiles.

Monday, August 21, 2017

I went for a drive, the wind in my hair, it was spectacular, I wished I didn't have to stop…just keep driving, keep going. I thought about how it will feel when I can no longer do that…I hope I'm strong enough to get through that chapter. I am, right? I think I will take Phoebe for a drive this week, let her enjoy the wind in her face too, she loves having her little face out the window, her ears blowing back. Tonight, I will try my wireless headset for music therapy to see if it will help me sleep.

Tuesday, August 22, 2017

Last night I put my head phones on with my Italian music, and I actually slept solid for 2 hours 10 minutes…then up for a bit and back to bed, slept until 4 AM, up for 15 minutes and slept till 6, feel so much more alert today. My head is hurting, but still I feel better, the pain is doable.

Thursday, August 24, 2017

Three nights of great sleep using music therapy, still exhausted but better able to get through the day, brain fog is much less. Finding I'm spending a lot of time getting ready for my move…my own home for the first time in almost three years, excited, apprehensive. While house sitting here, I figured out that I spend on average 22 hours a day alone. I can't let that kind of isolation continue, so once I'm settled, time for a new plan and a new way of life. I like days like today when my brain allows me some clarity of thoughts and actions…fully intend to enjoy this.

Friday, August 25, 2017

Well, today is a grand day, I actually slept from 11 PM to 6:40 this morning…Holy Hannah…you just can't imagine how that feels! I definitely know that the effects of the last TIA are lifting…yippee…my house sitting will end Monday or Tuesday and while preparing for my departure from here I am also getting ready for my move one week from today. It finally feels real…grateful to all those who have and are and continue to work hard to help make this happen. It will be unbelievable to open boxes and see things I haven't seen for a long time…it's exciting and I am so thankful that I am starting to rebound from this latest event in time to be able to enjoy the move. I am pacing things out to make sure it is all manageable for me.

My time here house/dog sitting has been good. TJ is such a special dog and I will miss him but I am sure he is so looking forward to seeing his family. Sunday I will spend the day mowing the lawn and enjoying the last bit of alone time.

Sunday, August 27, 2017

Last night I slept from 11 PM to 7 AM, so unbelievable! Taking a slow easy morning walk with my Phoebe, a relaxing phone chat with my sister, a lovely day. Tomorrow my two months of house sitting will be done. I will miss TJ, he is an incredibly beautiful dog, but I will come back to visit him. I will then house sit for Brent and Kay for the next five days during which time I will start the process of my move into my new apartment. I was there the other day and the work that Cara and Warren have done is incredible. It will be a lovely home for Phoebe and me.

It is an emotional time; it feels so surreal that in a few weeks it will be three years since my first big stroke and the beginning of the journey to the Dementia Diagnosis. It's been three years since I sold my home and to once again have my own place for Phoebe and me to settle; to have our own safe haven brings me to tears of happiness.

Wednesday, August 30, 2017

Yesterday I spent a lot of time thinking about the word 'terminal' and what that means to me. For most people when they hear the word, they think the person only has weeks or months to live. But for many of us with dementia…yes, my illness is classified as terminal…it is linked to the fact that the disease cannot be cured and the result will be death. Unlike people who are given only weeks or months, most of us have no time line. We are living with an illness that totally changes our lives; it continues to change as the disease progresses, there is no cure and we have no idea when the end will arrive.

A harder part of the equation is that, in the beginning, 'we don't look sick.' I am grateful that I don't look sick much of the time. However, after a TIA my face droops, my eyes are not right, my coordination and balance are all off for as many days as it takes to clear up.

Hearing a 'terminal' diagnosis creates a sense of urgency about the importance of really living, really enjoying time with people and amplifies all that is truly important for us. Maybe every one of us should, at some time, be told we are 'terminal' so we will take time to look inward because we are all born with an expiration date

.

Chapter Eleven

Thursday, August 31, 2017

I woke up feeling beyond excited. I get the keys to my new condo today at 1 PM! Today is the start of a new journey with this illness. I am regaining a very small but very important piece of all that is gone. I believe it will help thwart further decline, at least for now. I have been so blessed by all those who have helped me through the dark days and they have my deepest gratitude. Today I will take my computer, TV and such to the apartment so when Telus arrives early tomorrow, everything is there for them. At 8 AM the move will happen. Today feels good.

Saturday, September 2, 2017

I was exhausted at the end of yesterday; this morning I still feel tired. I managed to load and unload the 15-foot truck in two hours with the help of my friends; I'm very grateful that part's over. I'll take it slower now so I don't end up with another TIA.

I plan on taking Phoebe to see her new home for the first time this morning. I will bring her toy box; her chair is set up for her. Once I finish up today, I won't be able to do anything until after the kitchen and bathroom countertops go in then I can put those two rooms together. By the end of today the rest of the rooms will be complete. I will need to find a dresser and a small desk but it's not a priority. One thing I did realize yesterday was the full scope of how much is gone. Today will be a day of sitting in my home, processing it all and likely having tears of happiness flow. Then maybe I will shed tears of sadness for all I have lost and tears of gratitude for those who helped make this new chapter happen. On Wednesday my sister flies in and we leave on our girl's road trip. On returning, hopefully my countertops will be in.

Monday, September 4, 2017

Last night Phoebe and I spent our first night in our new home, slept well, I feel at peace here. I have set things up with a microwave and coffee maker; we can get by for a couple days. I'm glad I was well rested prior to the move or I think it would have been too much for me. I am learning my limits.

Wednesday, September 6, 2017

I've decided to do a memory wall, family, friends, places; I'm doing it in my guest room. My home feels very peaceful, it has calmness about it, the energy around here feels good. This was a move with great significance for me.

Wednesday, September 20, 2017

I haven't written for a bit; I was away to places that truly were good for the soul: peaceful, quiet, no traffic, no noise. Hearing only the sounds offered by Mother Nature made me think about how badly we need to have dementia care facilities built away from noisy centers with the space and ability to be outdoors.

It feels good to 'be home,' to have familiar things around me. My apartment is in a very quiet location beside a creek; it's perfect for us.

This trip has been good for me, it has taught me I am still capable of much and my sister has my back. There are more and more people who are treating me differently because of my illness. They no longer see me first; they see my illness first, and that is not good for me. I need to be treated as myself, I am still me, I make adjustments as I need to, but I'm the one who has to make them. Other people thinking they have to react differently because of my illness means my illness is winning. If you tell me you're adjusting or doing something differently because of my illness, I may understand but if you don't include me in the decision then you are taking away my ability to function at my fullest, you're putting my illness ahead of me.

I can no longer take on the responsibility of finding ways to help people come to terms with my illness. If they want to sit and laugh or cry with me about it, if they want to tell me they are afraid of what's coming, or they are sad, I can manage that. What I can't face is people treating me differently because THEY think it's best for me. I have no blinders on; until I can't figure out how to get through a day on my own, I will stay on my own. I hope if it's too hard, people can just say, "I love you my friend but I don't think I can do this." I can manage that.

Monday, September 25, 2017

My sleep the last two nights has not been good, I think I have to put my air conditioning back in for a while, my place is too warm with just the window open. I am enjoying my little space, it's a perfect location, very quiet, the green space that l look out on is so great. Other than going for my walks I haven't really left the house for the last couple days.

People always tell me I'm so strong. I just don't show the world the part of me that is scared; I cry my tears in private. I need that front because it makes me keep going. If I give in to those fears, the disease wins.

Tuesday, September 26, 2017

I still can't taste so I use a lot of sauces and spices to enhance flavor: herbs, hot, sweet, sour. When cooking, normally I taste to ensure the right mix of flavors; that has not been an option for me for some time. After settling into my little place and indulging my love of cooking, the challenges really became apparent. Now my tastes mean others may be subjected to foods that are a little more extreme than they are used to. I love cooking but at what point will I stop enjoying it because nothing tastes good? So please, if ever I am enjoying your hospitality at meal time, don't take offence if I doctor up my food. It's not your cooking; it's my lack of taste buds.

Thursday, September 28, 2017

I've had a couple of emotional days. I wanted to try to work a part time job for financial reasons and to stay socializing, but after my appointment with my doctor two days ago, I once again had to be very realistic and finally put the idea to rest. My doctor reminded me that it was only a month ago I was back at the hospital with another TIA, that they are happening all the time. I do as well as I do because I have the ability to adjust my days hour by hour or day by day as required. If I am working, I am setting myself up for more strokes, maybe more severe strokes, and the window they have been working so hard for me to have would be compromised. So, a decision had to be made, do I jeopardize my quality of life for money, or do I enjoy this window of time? It has taken two long hard years to get to a point where once again I am managing in my little home. I want to be able to maintain it for a long time; I want to enjoy my family, friends and little dog.

Saturday, September 30, 2017

The doctor wants to do more testing on my sleep/ apnea/ oxygen levels, so tonight, no CPAP machine, just the oxygen and the oximeter to see what happens and how I feel. Tomorrow night I will be testing with combination CPAP and oxygen; I can't slow the dementia if my brain is always starving for oxygen.

Friday, October 6, 2017

My sleep tests were really bad. The therapist who did them yesterday said that one in particular scared him; he had never seen anything like it. The episode lasted two hours. He said it was like my brain forgot to tell my lungs to breathe. He said this event was not a normal apnea type event, he doesn't really know what to say except there's more going on, and I need to get to a doctor. I know it sounds crazy but I sort of chuckled. Little does he know! One good thing is one night I am likely just not going to pull out of a bad episode. Considering what's ahead of me that would be a great way to go, peacefully, quietly, I wouldn't mind.

Now that I have been back in my little place for a month a lot more revelations have come to light. I cannot multi task, I cannot manage a dinner of more than 4 or five people, I cannot be out all day. After only a few hours my brain is exhausted. The more tired it is the more challenging it becomes to manage even small things.

I have my new little place so I can have my independence for as long as possible. I am really enjoying it but I did not get my old life back. I try to stay positive; I try to take and enjoy each day as it is. However, I am human, and sometimes it hits me and I cry and get angry and frustrated. I am happy in my little place with my dog, grateful to those who come to see me, for being able to spend time with family and friends and maybe I can't manage it as in the past but I still enjoy this new normal.

Monday, October 9, 2017

Thanksgiving! I had a nice quiet reflective day, a couple of nice walks, puttered in my safe little haven. The delivery of a plate of turkey dinner finished off a day of truly being grateful.

Yesterday I spend the morning at hospice house sitting with my friend's loved one during her final moments. I have always felt it an honor to do this. I just sat, being in the moment then stayed until the family had been notified. After, I went for a long walk to take time to refresh myself then spent a quiet day in reflection of my own life. I appreciate the offers to attend Thanksgiving dinners and am grateful for the invitations even though I can no longer attend large group settings. Receiving the invitation shows I am thought of, loved, and means more than anyone realizes.

Tuesday, October 10, 2017

I have gone from being a social butterfly to a person who still needs and wants social stimulation in smaller settings, without too much outside stimulation. It's a challenge and I can't expect others to change their lives to accommodate mine so I become the one that has to adjust and change. I am looking at becoming part of the Alzheimer's group, hopefully to meet some people who are younger. I don't feel like I fit in many places anymore and I don't enjoy feeling like I hinder others because it takes me longer to complete things, to find words during conversations, to explain myself. I was going to volunteer but I don't have the ability to do that. Even volunteer organizations want you to commit to a certain number of hours or days a week and commit for at least a year. That's impossible for someone like me. It becomes more difficult to find that socialization and stimulation but I will continue to search for the right fit for myself. In the meantime, I will keep talking to people when I am out for my walks.

Thursday, October 12, 2017

I have to go to Kelowna for a night or two of testing; I also will be having another MRI. Dr. Cunningham told me they had another conference and decided they wanted an MRI not a CT scan. I guess that was all decided after Dr. Pretorius saw me during the aftermath of my last significant TIA and couldn't do the testing he wanted to. He will do it later this month.

I used to be so strong in my English and spelling abilities but it's really slipping lately. I have to now ask Siri for help to spell many words.

Had coffee with my friend, Shelly, who I don't get to see often but enjoy whenever I do. Our conversations always do me good. She put into words for me something I have had trouble saying. Her words were, "Your only focus should be on doing and experiencing, nothing else." Thank you, it's what I am trying to do and have had difficulty explaining. She suggested I should put the photos of all my trips into albums and then have them made into photo books for later. I think it's a perfect idea, may need to recruit someone to help me with it, but I'm going to try.

Friday, October 20, 2017

I was reading a very interesting article by a doctor in New Zealand who specializes in dementia care. I am so glad there are doctors like him. I will be discussing some of what he talks about with my own doctors. He suggests when the disease has progressed to a certain point doctors should stop all other medications, like cholesterol, blood pressure, heart meds, and only give and focus on things that will provide comfort. Don't treat pneumonia; don't do surgeries for broken hips, etc. None of those things will change the outcome. Today I am still well enough to be treated but the day is coming when that will not be the case. Prolonging life should not be considered at a certain point; I would rather be able to die naturally without the 'doctoring' than have to endure living in any of our so called 'homes.'

Wednesday, October 25, 2017

A meeting with Community Futures gave me some hope yesterday. They are going to have their top man work with me on a few different things. I told them I'm not done! I still have things I am capable of doing, things I can contribute. I have read that the stigma around dementia creates the biggest challenges. People focus on the disabilities instead of the abilities still there. Sufferers are robbed of those abilities because they are ignored. I agree and if I do nothing then I too will be a victim of society putting me out to pasture. So, with Community Futures' guidance, November will find me busy putting together plans. "I am not done!" has become my new motto.

Thursday, October 26 2017

I had an appointment with my specialist yesterday. We talked about my frustrations with the stigma surrounding dementia and how even a lot of doctors struggle with that because their knowledge is limited. I told him I am in fight mode and he's happy I am.

We talked at length about dementia's impact on relationships and about how some people have slipped away, some have drastically changed, some have become even closer. He told me that although some people may think of me as stubborn, what I really am is very realistic and practical and that is helping me thrive when most would not. Being so realistic and practical allows me to let my friends be what they need to be. My practicality helps me know that my energy has to be invested in maintaining and taking care of myself and I have to let other people figure out how to work through how they feel towards me and my illness.

He did new testing, so the good news, I tested at 23 – yippee only one point lower than six months ago. I am maintaining.so happy! He said everything we are doing is helping this happen. We talked about the realistic and practical side of me that has put things into place that help me have a better quality of life: blister packs, reminders, setting myself up living close to everything I need. He said because I have that fight mode, that practical and realistic personality that he sees so seldom I am like a breath of fresh air. We talked about me doing the talk at Okanagan College about living with dementia and he thinks I should do as much of that as I can. He wants me to work with Community Futures to help find something that is meaningful to me. Saying 'I'm not done yet' will help overcome the barriers. It felt really good to be validated, to be encouraged, to know that although I can't change the outcome of the disease, I can choose how to live with it. I left feeling proud of myself, a feeling that too often eludes me these days.

Right after my meeting with the specialist I had to face something that came with a lot of sadness; I said goodbye to my beautiful little car. It has now gone to Richmond to be sold. I know it is the right thing to do but it is another of many tough choices I had to make. Today I will just allow myself to be sad about it. I may get another cheap run about car down the road but for now I will learn to be okay and be grateful that although I bought it for when I retired, I at least got to enjoy it for a time.

Book Three
Progress

Chapter Twelve

Monday, January 1, 2018

Today I start the Keto diet; it's supposed to be the best for the brain. Hopefully I can figure it all out. Sitting enjoying morning coffee, enjoying last day of Christmas twinkling lights, it's quiet, its peaceful, my body feels more rested, my vision is clear, no brain pain, oh so very grateful. I am hoping for more good days. It's hard to explain to people how exciting it is to have a day like most people have every day.

Tuesday, January 2, 2018

After being up for about an hour this morning I realized I had slept all night, a very rare phenomenon, and I was working through my tasks with ease. Then sitting having my coffee I thought back to two nights previous when I woke in the middle of night feeling an electrical jolt going down my right side, down my leg and out my foot. Since then I have had the two best days I have had in a couple months. Today I went to physio, then went walking with Phoebe for about two and a half hours. I bundled up, it was cold, but the air felt good. We stopped for a cup of tea along the way and I marveled at how clear my thoughts were. The woman from the Kelowna Alzheimer's Association called to say she had heard my interview on CBC. We talked about things that need to change to better suit those with dementia. I suggested that perhaps they could look at putting together a weekend seminar for younger people as our needs are different than those of Seniors. We need to find a way to have all of us connect easier. She encouraged me to keep using my voice to fight for change. It was nice to actually follow the conversation all the way through. I am so thankful for these clear days.

Thursday, January 4, 2018

Well that was a terrible night! Yesterday saw me getting a lot of things done, mostly paperwork. Since late last summer I have been trying to get

Pacific Blue Cross to cover part of the cost for a new oxygen concentrator as per my coverage. My present one quit working. I had arranged for a loaner at that time because I couldn't afford to pay full price for a new machine and I didn't want to spend money on a rental when I was going to buy. In early December, the supply company changed the agreement and charged me the full rental rate from the time they first loaned me the equipment because Blue Cross is still processing my request. I was sent a very large and unsuspected bill. They also lost the paperwork I had given them which they were supposed to give to Blue Cross in September but did not inform me until they presented the bill. I provided the paperwork again. My oxygen concentrator was picked up yesterday until such time as I can pay for it with the help of Blue Cross. The decision lay on me like a lead weight but I cannot afford to keep paying the rental amounts. I did get them to agree to look at crediting me the already paid fees towards the purchase price. They won't guarantee that will happen.

I also spent hours on the phone trying to speak to someone at Blue Cross; today I will try again. I am frustrated with our medical system. It is so draining. Chronically sick people should be using their energy to stay as well as possible and enjoy whatever 'good' amount of time they have. Yet they spend so much of it fighting for things they need.

I am fortunate that people near and far have helped ease my load by helping to cover that huge rental bill and pay for my physio (I have to pay for a set amount before Blue Cross takes over paying) so I didn't lose that as well. I am saddened by how quickly illness wipes out all your savings. The coverage we think we have is riddled with loop holes so the companies who take our money for years get out of paying for what we need. I had mortgage insurance, I had car loan insurance, I had extended health insurance, I had insurance on everything, but at the end of the day they have built in loop holes and you can't fight them when you're sick, so you pay out of your own pocket for things you thought were covered. So many people say, "Well you should have done this or that." Sometimes even when you do this and that it's not enough. When you can no longer go out and work or you don't have a partner who can bring in the extra income, it's a game changer.

What does it mean not having my oxygen? My brain needs it to function in a healthy manner. How long before more irreversible damage is done? I don't know. Maybe it's time for me to consider stopping all the treatments and just enjoy myself for whatever time I can. My heart is heavy today.

After being on hold for nearly an hour I finally spoke to someone at Blue Cross who was able to say, "I'm terribly sorry for this; unfortunately, there is nothing I can do. Keep checking your account to see if your problem has been dealt with. The department who makes the decisions doesn't talk to people." I again stated the need and he said he could try to send them an email and have them respond to him. I suggested that he might want to let them know that if they can't find me a human that can actually get this dealt with then, perhaps, I could go to Global News.

All of a sudden it was, "No, please don't do anything, I will call you back today, I will get some answers for you." Why do I have to take such drastic measures to get the help I should routinely receive? Now I wait. I am fortunate I have a good support team and I am strong willed by nature. It breaks my heart when I know there are people who have given up fighting the system because they don't have the same perseverance I do. They are the reason I talk about these frustrations so people understand how challenging it is to be sick and have to deal with all these unnecessary struggles.

Friday, January 5, 2018

There is always sunshine amidst the storm. Yesterday afternoon and this afternoon, silver linings abound. Through the determination of a couple of human angels, Richard and Cindy, who showed up at my door yesterday and rescued me when I was overwhelmed and drowning, allowing me to have a melt down until I could laugh again. They then found me a temporary solution through a man I didn't know. Andy, you are my silver lining today and for days to come. Thank you from the bottom of my heart for stepping up to help, for providing me an oxygen concentrator to use until my issues can be resolved. It is an unmeasurable gift. I hope I get the opportunity to meet you one day and give you a hug of thanks. Tomorrow the oxygen concentrator will come, giving me quality again. My head hurts so bad today, but at the same time my heart is flooding.

To Marijon, I thank you for just stepping in and quietly helping. You are one of the angels walking the earth who goes with me for walks and talks and makes plans to spend time with me: you understand the struggle so well. To all the friends and family who are just always there, I am grateful.

Some wonder why I write so often. I write so people have, I hope, a better understanding of the challenges associated with living with dementia. I hope it makes other sufferers feel like they don't need to be ashamed, to hide away. In some small way, I hope to make a difference every day I am able I to use my voice. Many people reach out to me from many corners of the country with private messages about their journeys or the journeys of their loved ones. I am always honored. I also hope to find younger people living with dementia, so that we can be supports for each other, learn and share together, and try to make a real difference because our needs differ from the older population living with dementia.

Saturday, January 6, 2018

Seems for some reason I am now writing at night when I have always written in the morning. Last night wasn't a good night, I've been exhausted again.

Today I joined an organization called Dementia Alliance International. It is for people with dementia. They have coffee time chats, educational seminars, sharing of experiences and ways to improve dementia living. Here in Canada we have all fallen into this false sense of security that everything that can be done is being done. Our willingness to be complacent leaves us falling short and falling behind. My first live session will be Thursday; I am hoping to find it very engaging.

I was in my kitchen today after the loaner oxygen concentrator arrived and all of a sudden, I felt like I got hit by a train. It was like a neon sign flashing at me "It doesn't matter what you do you're never getting better!" There I was preparing my Keto dinner to feed my brain all the healthy fats it wanted, had been for my walk, was excited to have the oxygen concentrator. The roller coaster of emotions never stops. My Aricept medication restarts today so hoping in a few days I will be stable again. Off to bed.

Dr. Cunningham went on vacation and had another doctor cover for him. This doctor decided I had been given the wrong medication and took away my Aricept. She replaced it with a drug that was not as effective but I had to go through the escalation process before I could stop taking it.

Sunday, January 7, 2018

Wow, I had a good night's sleep thanks to my stranger friend, Andy. Hoping for some clearer, better days ahead.

Monday, January 8, 2018

I went to bed early last night: 9 PM. I wanted to be on my oxygen. My body must have needed it; I slept undisturbed until 6:15 this morning.

Although, overall, I am happy for each day, I am increasingly frustrated with the lack of opportunities available for people with dementia. I read a lot about the disease, I have applied to be in a couple trials but so far have not been accepted. I know and feel so many changes in my life, many things I am forgetting. It feels good when something triggers a memory of some enjoyed incident. It's strange to live always waiting for the next step in the disease process to manifest itself. My body is so able; from the outside it usually looks great. If someone spent a week with me, they would be shocked at how difficult managing one whole day is. Yet it is the simplest and most basic things that bring me happiness and fulfillment now: a cup of coffee or meal, someone coming by for a visit or a walk, a phone call to chat. My needs and wants are minimal and sometimes when I look around and see the unhappiness of people who are so over-stressed trying to have it all, do it all, I think, I used to be one of those people. This horrible illness has given me the gift of removing all that from my life. I have to be friends with it and understand how blessed I truly am.

Tuesday, January 9, 2018

Yesterday, after writing, I went for a walk with Phoebe, came home and started puttering around the house. A couple of huge lightning bolts struck my brain hard enough I ended up in bed for the rest of the day. Sometimes when I have these events I try to keep going, sometimes I rest in my chair to let it dissipate, very rarely do I let it put me to bed. I'm feeling better again this morning. It's difficult for others to understand how one minute you seem great and the next minute you can barely put two and two together.

Wednesday, January 10, 2018

Today was like someone hit the reset button: slept well, went to physio, came home and went out walking with a friend for a couple hours then home to take my dog out for another stroll for an hour. Late in the day I received a call from my friend at Pacific Blue Cross who promised to call back. He has involved his supervisors into trying to get some coverage towards my oxygen concentrator. He needed a little more information which I gave him. That shows you really have to keep fighting and pushing to get the type of care you deserve. It scares me to think what life would look like for me if I didn't have the ability to advocate so strongly for myself. In the past, I've asked for referrals to other specialists when I felt I needed new eyes. My doctor never doubted that there was something serious going on with me and continued working until we got the answers. I have been hearing of so many struggling in many of the same ways trying to get answers, trying to get in to see specialists. I want awareness to the fact that whether it's dementia or any other illness, people should not have to struggle so hard to receive proper and timely care.

Sunday, January 14, 2018

Sarah from CBC sent me a message about an upcoming program she created which will be on TV tonight. It's an interesting watch. For all the times I wish I wasn't alone, in many ways I am thankful that my illness does not have to devour anyone else's life. Yes, I need the love and support of all my family and friends, but they don't have to live with me 24 hours a day. They are not consumed and swallowed up by my illness. Caregivers did it out of love and a feeling of responsibility; that's how the world used to work.

I have to prepare myself so my plans are very solid. I will make changes as necessary; I will stay independent for as long as possible. To ensure no unnecessary interventions are done my doctor will adhere to my written wishes. Until then the most important thing is to try to stay engaged with people, to continue to learn new things, to experience new adventures however small. I still feel, understand, sense the world, and have much to contribute. I am still determined to end up with a part time job, still looking for that person or place who will take a chance to see what I have to offer.

Tuesday, January 16, 2018

I feel like I am back at a level spot. My medications that help my blood flow and heart work properly make such a huge difference in how I function. The difference good blood/oxygen flow to my brain makes is remarkable. (Once I was on my combination of good CPAP machine and oxygen, life improved again for me. The combination improved my sleep, which means I had better days, my cognitive abilities were better and held for longer periods of time). Still, I'm having more difficulty retrieving information I know I have in my brain. That is something I can work around and most people won't notice. People with dementia get very good at that because we know our own struggles.

I am trying very hard to stay connected but am finding I am spending more and more time alone. Other than walking my dog or going to physio I spend days and days at home, something I have never done, and actually I am not minding it. I'm enjoying the quiet where I don't have to work so hard to meet someone's expectations. Last week I spend a great deal of time alone, this week I have a lot of appointments, a lunch date, a coffee date, volunteering at the good food box, an overnight stay on Thursday at Kelowna General Hospital, and an overnight to Kamloops on Saturday (thanks to June).

I am really missing driving right now, it was such a hard thing to give up, yet I know it was the right thing. Although I still have my license and am hoping this spring to be able to rent a car for a couple days so I can tootle around, I am managing without driving. Yesterday I missed it so much I cried. The other day I looked in the mirror and stood there thinking who are you and where has Christine gone? Off to the races I go. Time to get ready for my first of many appointments this week.

First my specialist and I went over the CT scan report then we looked at the scan of my brain, frame by frame, so I could see the damaged areas. It is hard to look at but not looking at it, having blinders on so to speak, would be worse for me. Knowing, seeing, understanding, is all part of helping my fight. I can't do all I can for myself if I don't accept, learn and understand what's happening.

We then talked about my writing, my being willing to speak and try to advocate for people with dementia, it's my purpose now. He said it's actually a job, and likely the most important one I've ever done or will do. It will help keep me independent and thriving for a long time.

He asked me how my family and friends were dealing with my illness. It's a hard question for me to answer: some are struggling, some are in denial, some have disappeared altogether. We talked about the importance of staying connected to people who will help me have my best possible life in ways best for me. There is a responsibility on their part to stay engaged, to educate themselves on how to accept my illness, to communicate their worries and fears, to be able to ask me questions, and to educate others around me. I can only work through how it affects them if they share with me. I have accepted the plate handed me; I cannot be responsible for others coming to terms with it. As the doctor said, I am not an alien, I am still me, with some changes, some differences. If people can learn to enjoy my good days, there is still a lot of love and laughter left inside me. I really enjoy those who can laugh and cry with me.

He specifically asked how it feels when people think they can say and do things 'because I won't remember anyway.' I found that an interesting question. People do say things that are hurtful. They are making light of my illness and that I hope to see change. You don't say to someone with cancer, "Oh well, that's okay, I'm like that too." People joke all the time about dementia, whether friends or the local clerk at the grocery store. Sometimes I want to scream, "No, you're not having a dementia moment, you have no idea!" I don't because they are talking from a place of ignorance and I have to focus on educating people who truly are interested in understanding.

He says as a doctor, watching me accept and find ways to live and thrive with my illness instead of allowing it to pull me under is a true inspiration to him. It was a visit (much better word than appointment) that was informative, confirming, uplifting, and validating. I am, in his words, doing remarkably well considering the blow I was dealt. I am grateful for my doctors.

Chapter Thirteen

Wednesday, January 17, 2018

I am not walking as much the last few days because the streets and sidewalks are too icy. This greatly effects my sleep patterns, which have not been good for two nights.

One of the things that I really want people to understand is that 'I am not suffering from dementia; I am living with dementia.' I choose to dance its dance the best I can. I want to thrive, to be the best version of me in spite of all the messed up, jumbled up bits and pieces that are my day. I choose to embrace this journey so I can be happy and smile and laugh and learn new things. Today I am doing my orientation to be a volunteer with the Patient Voice Network. It is another way I can stay engaged and try to make a difference.

Thursday, January 18, 2018

Today was a phenomenal day! From my early morning reminder text that it was good food box volunteer day (I had so forgot!), to being left with enough time before my next volunteer commitment to enjoy a cup of tea with Tara, to the chance meeting with an old friend, it became an uplifting and inspiring day that made me excited to be alive. What an inspiring young lady and I hope for more opportunities to be engaged in such uplifting conversation.

Then I was off to my second volunteer position with the Patient Voices Network (a British Columbia Ministry of Health Initiative). Today was all about what and how to move forward to meet the needs of seniors in our community. I had a chance to speak about the gaps that have befallen the younger set and those of us that are striving to maintain a quality of life and remain independent. There is a shortfall of resources available to us and little assistance to access what there is. Many people from various levels were represented at this meeting: doctors, social workers and various groups and organizations dealing with various aspects of dementia. A wonderful man sought me out; he heads North Okanagan Mental Health and is working to cross over to Facilities (managing the buildings). Me having dementia was of great interest to him; we had an incredible conversation. He gave me his card and asked me to contact him next week so we can talk further.

I hope to speak to the Quality Review Board of Interior Health, they will be in contact within a week and want to hear the good and bad of my experiences and my suggestions for change. I look forward to that opportunity. As the day winds down, I am amazed that for all this disease has taken from me, how many wonderful people it has put in my path and the many opportunities that I have yet to complete. Sometimes the disease itself becomes the silver lining.

I am now tucked in at Kelowna General Hospital, feeling like Hannibal Lecter, hooked up for my brain scanning, breathing, heart testing. Oh, what fun it is.

Friday, January 19, 2018

Last night I endured some of my tests sitting at Tim Horton's in Orchard Park Mall. I had the pleasure of having a nice young man from India guide me through them. He brought me there at the end of his shift as there was nowhere open in the hospital to get coffee. Today June is bringing me home and tomorrow taking me to see friends. I'm excited to see the Kamloops gang. So grateful for a week of feeling and managing so well.

It hit me like a ton of bricks at just how small my world has become, how long it has been since I have been out of the perimeters that I walk or bus. Not driving has shrunk my world in ways I hadn't even realized until today. I have been robbed of satisfying that gypsy in me that has been prominent my whole life. Now I have to figure out how to still feed it without a vehicle of my own.

Sunday, January 21, 2018

Yesterday was slow paced and restful. I was able to enjoy an evening that was truly about visiting, about being in the now with each other, no cell phones going off, just the enjoyment of conversations and laughter with good friends. Today I will visit with another couple who have been long time friends and then head for home. Thanks to June for enabling me.

Monday, January 22, 2018

I woke up feeling sick about a statement made by a bright young woman who is taking a care aid course. Through no fault of her own, she made a statement about how people with dementia have brains that are shriveling up. She said that what you do for them doesn't matter because they don't know or won't remember anyway. I was so taken aback! This shows the lack of understanding and knowledge of the people who teach those doing face-to-face care. They are teaching outdated and disproved material. Because this young lady is so bright, she will excel at whatever field she chooses and will learn to question some of the things she is being taught.

But this really speaks volumes about why I must work so hard in my advocating. We are so much more than the disease, at every stage, and it truly is time for people to realize that. I used to speak to care-aid students through Sprott Shaw and OUC Kelowna. I must now work to have changes made to the curriculum being taught in this province. Again, I will reach out to those I know in the education sector who can help me have a voice within those walls. Thank you, young lady, for showing me another place where changes need to be made. My motto of I'M NOT DONE could not be stronger than it is these days; my purpose is clear. The reason I was chosen to have this disease is clear.

Tuesday, January 23, 2018

Wow, did I sleep! A wonderful day yesterday spent with a nursing friend, Barbara. We had fun getting the details worked out for the Gateby/Noric luncheon. I used to organize all those things without batting an eye, couldn't do it without her help this year. Later today I will be back on the advocating trail. When I am on a good brain stretch, I try to use that time to get some productive hours in on pending projects.

I just watched the 7th episode of the documentary 'Broken Brain' and suddenly had a light bulb moment. This is exactly what I've been doing since the beginning of January: switching my diet around, doing some pieces quickly others more slowly, starting my day by adding a tablespoon of Coconut oil to my coffee, eating lots and lots of healthy fats, no sugar, very few carbs from our traditional sources, instead getting them from veggies. I am not perfect at it yet. No TIAs for the last bit; feeling really good. I know there is no cure, but what if by making the changes I can maintain where I am? What if it's helping to get rid of the inflammation in my body and particularly in my brain? Can I buy myself a couple more good years? I am going to pay attention and see if it's just coincidence or if by eating this way I am truly helping fight the disease. I keep finding ways to empower myself!

Thursday, January 25, 2018

I was startled awake about 2:45 AM by one of the dreaded lightning bolts flashing through my head. The electrical charge it creates is painful, then it sends my heart racing, so it takes a while to let everything settle down and I can once again sleep. Of course, not everyone with dementia has these types of brain events, it is quite an individualized disease in many ways. There is no history of the disease in my family, but there is huge history of heart and stroke issues, some have died as early as their forties and up to their early seventies. My mother was one of the longer living ones at 80. I believe it was her attitude about life that kept her with us that long. I have cardiovascular disease, small vessel disease and a history of TIAs. These conditions cause the lightning bolts.

Today I have my first live coffee chat via the internet with Dementia Alliance International. I will be meeting by video with other people from around the world who are living with dementia. This is a worldwide organization which advocates for change. At this point Canada has only a small number of people within this organization.

DAI is joining a World Alzheimer's Conference this summer in Chicago which will be presenting to doctors, health care providers, pharmaceutical companies, volunteers, clinicians, scientists, etc. I wish I could go. I know it would connect me to so many that could really help in my fight for better treatment and care of people with dementia right here at home. I am baffled that Canada is so far behind so many other countries, especially in ways related to patients' everyday health and wellbeing. We should be world leaders.

Friday, January 26, 2018

I believe the change to eating more Keto based foods is really helping my inflammation and that multiplies my good brain days.

Yesterday, while chatting with my Dementia Alliance International group I was asked if I would be interested in putting forward an abstract to speak at the World Alzheimer's Conference in July. I will put it forward. It is another and maybe most important piece of advocating I can do. I felt empowered and inspired. There is so much we can learn from each other. If I have to have this disease, I will use my voice to help improve things for people living with it. This weekend I will be starting the abstract; there is a selection process. I need to attend this conference, to learn, to meet so many others living with dementia. I can bring back so much to help make things better right here in my community. DAI may be the organization that will give us a voice and empower us because it is for people with dementia, not the caregivers, not the loved ones, but those of us living with it. I will be scrimping and saving so, in July, I can attend what will likely be one of the most important conferences of my life.

Saturday, January 27, 2018

Last evening, I told my sister-in-law, Kay, my reasoning for fighting for the right to still work. I know my disability pension will not allow me to make much, which is wrong on so many levels I can't even begin to list them all. It's not really about the money. Yes, my disability pension is not enough, but more than that I want the social interaction, I want to feel good about myself. When my doctor suggested that perhaps I should consider assisted living, that just made me fight harder to find ways to maintain my life. From learning about eating the Keto way so my brain gets what it's starving for, to my Pilates/physio three times a week, to walking each and every day no matter the weather, to setting up my little apartment with all I need to make my life easier, I have worked hard.

It can be challenging at times, living alone without those built-in support systems. By the way, I believe a lot of people take for granted their support systems. Even the simplest little things make a difference, like having that person who will bring you a coffee or tea if you're not feeling well, or change the light bulb for you so you don't have to use a chair to reach. When you're it, you're on all the time. Most people have no idea how much their support person actually does for them and when you are on your own you don't really think too much about it, you know you just do what you have to do. If you have any type of illness or disability, you quickly understand the gift and importance of that person, be it a spouse, roommate or family member. Having none of those means I fight harder. Maybe that's the thing that will help me battle this disease and stay at this stage for longer.

Tuesday, January 29, 2018

I'm sitting in bed drinking my coffee this morning, looking out my bedroom window at the snow-capped trees, enjoying how pretty they are all covered in white. I shoveled my parking spot out last night, so if I have visitors, I'm ready.

Today I have to go see Dr. Cunningham and get the results of my tests I had done in Kelowna last week. I'm not expecting anything new. In a sense, I have made friends with my dementia. I let it motivate me, give me drive and purpose. All changes become part of the daily dance. I am functioning well right now and I don't take that for granted. My energy is so precious, I baby it, take care of it, use it for things that are truly important. Who knows, maybe at some point I will meet someone willing to share my journey. This illness has led me to some incredible people from around the world, I am blessed to have them in my life and all that they offer in friendship, to learn, share and support each other. So today my silver linings are my Dementia Alliance International family.

Wednesday, January 30, 2018

Yesterday, while out with a girlfriend, we talked about the ways people treat me differently since my diagnosis. She has noticed how some of my friends don't interact with me anymore. There are, on a weekly basis, people asking her about 'Dementia Christine.' She has difficulties in understanding why people wouldn't just come to visit and ask me the questions. They fear the illness and don't stop to think that I am aware they avoid me. They come up with excuses for not seeing me in person. It's hurtful.

These people won't have an honest conversation with me about how I struggle living with this illness because they always see my dementia first. Some dislike the fact that I'm not behaving the way they perceive I should be, that I am staying independent, that I am actively trying to change people's perception of my illness. I actually feel sorry for them because they are missing out on some very real and wonderful times with 'Person Christine.' I don't have a choice but they have a choice about how to respond to me and my illness.

Chapter Fourteen

Thursday, February 1, 2018

I'm feeling better and stronger. People tell me all the time, "You're so brave." I'm not brave! There are so few options to help me live up to my full potential, very few ask if they can assist with that achievement. I choose not to accept that. I felt very alone in my fight to advocate for myself and others until, after extensive research, I found Dementia Alliance International. I live with my dementia, just like people live with Cancer or Diabetes or MS, and I deserve to be treated with the same amount of dignity.

Friday, February 2, 2018

The weeks and days seem to be disappearing so quickly, it's as though I can't keep up, it takes so much more time for me to complete tasks or get myself organized and ready in the mornings.

I am feeling quite proud of myself; my abstract submission to present at the World Dementia Conference as part of my Dementia Alliance International group was completed and submitted yesterday. For many, that may not seem like a big deal but for me who now writes words backwards, who writes but is not able to put thoughts in proper order, who can no longer make sense of proper structure, and who can't stay focused, it is a huge accomplishment.

I could not have completed it without my lovely sister-in-law, Kay, taking time to check over my work and sitting with me to ensure it was put together properly. She understands the importance to my quality of life these kinds of things are. They challenge my brain to create new pathways, they give me purpose. She is my silver lining for having patience when my brain can't process something, for being able to laugh with me at the backward words. I am grateful she has chosen to embrace my illness, join me in my journey, and help in ways she is able. We don't want our lives taken over because people think we are no longer capable, we need assistance and support with the areas we struggle with so we can continue to do all the things we are capable of.

I am proud of myself for striving and pushing to do something I've not done before, for keeping growing despite my dementia. This disease may be robbing me of much, but it also is giving me new direction, bringing new people into my life to share journeys together, giving me the opportunity to stand up and help make changes in how dementia is perceived and treated.

Saturday, February 3, 2018

My choice to start living the Keto diet came after three long, hard years with my illness, researching what my diagnosis meant to my body and understanding all the newest information about treatment. The latter included the importance of proper nutrition. This diet uses high fats, protein and low carbs to fight inflammation and the use of high fat snacks to super charge the brain. Reading of the astounding results around the world for people with dementia, I started my eating regimen on the 2nd of January. Every day I see improvements in my ability to focus, to hold conversations, to complete tasks, to have more sustained energy. I still have to be careful not to overexert but overall there is a vast improvement. I follow a lot of the Keto plan with some variables. This is not a cure but if it gives me better cognitive awareness, I can be independent longer and maintain a good quality of life. I am not interested in this diet to lose weight, I am interested because this change in what we are feeding our bodies is one that is proven in the scientific and medical world.

Monday, February 5, 2018

I just finished an 18 hour fast, it was my first one since switching to the Keto plan, I must say I thought it would be difficult but it really wasn't at all, I never felt hungry. I had my breakfast then at 11 AM switched to liquid only. I have no headache, slept well, still not feeling hungry, so just drinking my bullet coffee. It's amazing how I don't have the cravings for things now, no longer wake each night to have a snack. The biggest improvements for me are NO significant TIAs, decrease in brain fog, cognition improved, ability to focus improved. I believe Dr. Bredesen has given all of us with dementia something to be hopeful about. How long will these improvements last? I have no idea what time frame it will work for, but each day it does it is worth the effort to do it. I am truly fortunate that my doctor is willing to look at anything that may be of help. If I keep feeling as well as I am, I won't have to fear my next level of testing in April. I also didn't realize how important it is to be connected with others who share many of the same challenges and triumphs, another key to maintaining our wellbeing. Having the ability to chase a little dream or two again sure feels good.

Wednesday, February 7, 2018

This morning I am bright and alert, slept a solid 6.5 hours, not up once, so the diet seems to be helping my sleep patterns as well. I have to be my own guinea pig, monitor my own results, be my own test study. I am so blessed to have my Dementia Alliance International Brain Hub family that is also walking this road, sharing information about what is working what is not.

Yesterday I was able to contact my pension plan and this time was actually able to process the information he gave me. The last two days have seen me experimenting in the kitchen again, with new recipes and new ways of cooking. I sit in amazement at the fact that in one month I have seen such remarkable differences.

Friday, February 9, 2018

This new part time job which I have worked so hard to get, is creating stress, and challenges for me and it hasn't even started yet. The job is being a hostess in a restaurant, but the company has buried me in courses that they want me to complete. I finished several last weekend and thought I was done; now I have many more. Some days my brain doesn't want to process the content and I still, at times, put letters and numbers backwards which changes the outcome of the tests. Is this position the right choice for me? Will I be able to manage a scheduled job? Right now, I am managing great because I can adjust what I am doing depending on how I am functioning moment to moment. If I am struggling, I can stop, rest, go back to the task when my brain is functioning better. This looks like a job that could end up being much more than I anticipated. I'll spend the weekend trying to get through these tests then I'll make a decision to keep going or go look for something a little less stressful.

Although my cognitive awareness is so much better, I am becoming acutely aware of the areas where there is no improvement. For example, I am again following recipes, being able to change them as in the past to put my own spin on them but I have no recollection of when I last worked or when I was formally diagnosed. I have bigger gaps of memory than I realized. I do remember some odd things, like when I had a bad fall living up North and went by ambulance to have a brain scan done. The neurologist showed me the scan and said, "You have an absolutely beautiful brain!" No one tells me that anymore when reviewing my scans! I think my brain is still beautiful, it's like the rest of me, bruised, battled and scarred from life's struggles but still beautiful.

Sunday, February 11, 2018

There are many people that think they know and understand dementia either because of the work they do in care facilities or because they have known someone with a family member who struggled with the final stages. When someone they know is diagnosed, that's the first place their mind set takes them. If people were more willing to toss that flawed belief system aside, people living with dementia would have a much better quality of life and families wouldn't try to hide them from society.

When you side-step a person with dementia because: (a) you are seeing the disease not the person so you believe we don't understand or we will forget, or (b) you think you are doing us a favor by making decisions without our input, you are making us invisible, telling us we have no worth and taking away the abilities we have left. Society needs to start seeing us as we are; we still have the ability to be involved and engaged. We should be included in making decisions, we are still capable of telling people how we feel and what we need.

When dementia patients are placed in care facilities, they are stripped of every last ability they have; they are not even allowed to pour themselves a coffee! This is warehousing them. I said when I worked in such a facility that we were doing things wrong. I can tell you from the other side that I feel this even more strongly. People think they are being kind but because they don't know how to accept me with my dementia, they find excuses to not include me, or walk away from the friendship, or in any number of ways take away my abilities by not acknowledging them. One thing dementia does is increase all your other senses so you feel the rejection and it sucks. I have heard and seen it written many times: we are described as 'victims.' No! We have dementia, we don't want your sympathy, we want your help to change how we are perceived, we want your help to be included, we want your help to enjoy ourselves just like everyone else.

Monday, February 12, 2018

I can't remember the last time I had a TIA…Wow, my brain must be happy; I haven't had to get up and go through my questions about who I am or where I am. Whether anyone believes this is the right way I should eat simply doesn't matter because I have renewed hope for better days.

On a sadder note: after all my struggles with written tests I was told I could have the job of part-time dishwasher if I wanted it. I politely refused. I want a job where I can interact with people.

Saturday, February 17, 2018

I lose many minutes of the day, it feels like I just got up then I'm going to bed. What I've done throughout the day is filed in that cabinet in the back room of my brain, maybe never to be pulled out again. My brain is being very selective about what it wants to keep and what it puts into storage. I am so very thrilled that my noticeable TIAs have stopped. No lightning bolts or super charged electrical currents go pulsing through my head. The great thing is that the Keto diet is all natural.

Sunday, February 18, 2018

My heart feels heavy today, for which I have no explanation except to say that at times people look at me, they see the face that is shown to the world, the presentable one. They think, 'It's not that bad; she looks like she's doing fine.' They truly have no idea how much I actually struggle, how challenging it is to get up and fight for another day.

Sometimes I wonder why I spend so much energy trying to make my illness bearable for others, why I try to make it easier on them. I guess, in part, because I have already had to face so many losses, they keep mounting up, some are friendships and even family so we do everything we can to make our illness easier for those who still remain. Out of fear of more loss? Maybe, I am not sure. Some time ago I told some friends that one day soon I would like a girls' night out, tucked away where we could laugh, cry, let it all out. It never happened, maybe because I didn't organize it, I don't know, maybe because it wasn't important enough to them. Just because I'm viewed as strong and resilient doesn't mean I don't need people, that I don't have times where I feel like I'm drowning. So today my heart feels heavy.

Monday, February 19, 2018

Yesterday I took the day off, put my headphones on and listened to my music, did a lot of reading and research, played with my dog. Sometimes I need to quiet my outside so I can listen to the quiet that speaks in my heart.

One question came to me: even though I have dementia and even though it's terminal, shouldn't I be sitting down and figuring out how I want whatever is left of my life to look like? If someone has cancer, everything that can be done is done to ensure that person gets to do as many things as they can. Why is it when it's dementia it's treated so differently? Is it because there is not straight line from start to finish? Is it because people don't think it's as bad, or worse that we aren't capable of enjoying the experiences?

Yesterday I wanted to think about my life. I have people say, "Why don't you move closer to your family?" The reality is that they are all busy with their own lives and I have no interest in being an imposition on anyone. If helping is done out of feelings of obligation or because they think it's expected, then it is no longer being done from the heart and being on the receiving end doesn't feel good. I would like to see them more often; maybe visiting a couple times a year would be nice.

I also stay here because of my great doctors. In all honesty, if I truly decided to be somewhere else, they could help me in my quest for suitable replacements. As for my friends the same holds true for them as for family. So, the big question for me over the coming months: how do I reshape my life and what do I want it to look like? What keeps coming to me is that I want to be near the water…

Tuesday, February 20, 2018

I am very excited that I am being given the opportunity to do a presentation, through my involvement as a Patient Voices Network Partner, to the Interior Health Board. I will do my presentation on June 18th in Kelowna. They put a call out earlier this year for submissions and I put one forward.

This is extremely important; every time I get the opportunity to speak, I change how people view and treat those of us living with dementia. This opportunity I will not take lightly, and as a member of Dementia Alliance International, will work to represent those living in BC and Canada well. "Nothing about us, without us."

Busy days lie ahead getting ready for this and the International Conference in Chicago. Fund raisers will happen and as things get rolling I will ask family and friends to help.

Chapter Fifteen

Wednesday, February 21, 2018

If I could just figure out what's causing me to have nose bleeds several times a day! They've been ongoing for a couple weeks. I thought maybe a humidifier was the answer but apparently not.

I am actually looking forward to my next testing to see what the scores show for improvement. This Protocol is giving me results far exceeding what I hoped for. In the next few years, many people will be diagnosed with some type of dementia who will be younger than me. Years ago, people that were diagnosed with Multiple Sclerosis had to learn to live well in spite of their illness. We now have to do the same.

Thursday, February 22, 2018

Yesterday I had so much fun! My friend June came from Kelowna, took me around to different car lots and I went test driving new cars. Driving felt so good! It was such a big part of who I was; I miss it more than anyone could possibly understand. I hope if I keep feeling this good and if my testing in April is stable, maybe, by fall, I can find a way to have a little runabout car again. I have not driven since October, it was exhilarating, I could feel it to my bones, that pure joy I always had. Driving was about the wide-open spaces, discovering something new just around the corner, taking life in. When I put my hands on the wheel yesterday, I just sat there and breathed deep, remembering those feelings. It was a great reminder that I am still here. Oh, to have a car again, it's a dream and it's a hope.

Also, my friend Dallas called from Maine, his calls are always a welcomed spot in my day, always a laugh to be had despite our dementia or maybe because of it. Either way I am so grateful for new friendships forged. They make one feel less alone and better understood.

Saturday, February 24, 2018

Had an early morning coffee chat with Dallas; we have great and sometimes very deep spiritual conversations. He left me with my heart feeling good and feeling understood. I have been thinking more and more that I don't fit very well into mainstream society. I am happy within myself and the journey I am on; I am not hiding my illness. If I bring it to people's attention, they often become offended and yet it should be me who is offended by the things they say.

Not fitting in is not something that worries me, I am aware of it, I am happy enough to allow myself the ability to live more fully within myself. I am content, likely more at peace with how I am than I ever have been. Sometimes I miss the one I used to see in the mirror but I try to embrace the one who is here now. Some time ago, while chatting with my friend Dallas, I had said, "I like dementia." It allows us freedom to accept ourselves as we are, not what society thinks we should be. We are able to go into a deeper spiritual part of ourselves.

Sunday, February 25, 2018

I have been feeling and functioning so much better since starting Dr. Bredesen's Protocol. It takes me back to many conversations with my mother. She always said, "Don't cut all that fat off, you need it. Don't eat that low fat, no fat stuff, it's not good for you." Oh Mom, how wise you were! I used to call you a Witch Doctor with all your home-made remedies. You saved my life as a child when the doctors couldn't. I had severe pneumonia four times and traditional medicine wasn't helping so you and grandma took me home, made me homemade herbal medicines, rubbed me down and I survived. You also taught me doctors have their place but I have the responsibility to keep myself healthy. You taught me never to just believe what I hear or follow the status quo without researching the facts.

Your wisdom still serves me well. Thanks to you I think outside the box; I'm open to other points of view and newly breaking knowledge. I am one of many with dementia who are having success with the protocol. People like myself, those willing to try out new science that goes against what we were taught, are the ones who will bring new knowledge to the forefront. Without this we have nothing; no traditional methods have helped much.

My other thoughts over the weekend have been about my emotional wants. How can I ever hope to find a relationship with a man? I feel I still have a lot to offer. I suppose the possibility will just have to sit in the back corner of my mind where it usually is. Every once in a while, it pops up and I ponder the way to work around it then I laugh and think I can just see it..."Hi, I'm Christine, I live with dementia, how do you like me so far?" I get this funny mind picture of someone running for their life! Deeply sad.

Monday, February 26, 2018

Something else has happened twice now and the first time I thought I was imagining it. My sense of taste was gone for the last two years, no taste sensations except very sour or very sweet. Not being into sweets, I was always zesting my food with tart or very spicy seasonings. Someone would ask how my meal was, I would always say really good or great, when truly I had no idea how it actually tasted. That was easier than trying to explain.

Fast forward to a few weeks ago, I am once again able to follow recipes and cook again. One day I sat down to eat the meal I prepared and ended up in tears because I could actually taste some flavors. I seemed to slip back, to not tasting things, then I made raspberry fat bombs. I could taste them and the lemon ones on some days. June took me out for lunch, I ordered a beef Thai Salad and just about jumped up and danced on the table when those taste sensations came through. Another improvement, another victory.

Wednesday, February 28, 2018

After much deliberation, with the clear knowledge and understanding that at any time things could go south again, I have purchased a small, second hand car. If I'm having a rough patch, I won't drive but being able to drive again is a gift I cannot even put into words. I have not even been able to get to Costco in Kelowna for five months now because no one has offered to take me. I will cherish the gift of driving for what freedom it gives to me and my little dog. I have already faced the loss of it, I have already learned that I can and will survive when I have to give it up for good, but for now I will enjoy this time. When people with different illnesses go into remission, they are encouraged to go out and do things they enjoy. If I am finding things that are helping me have my own sort of remission, I should be encouraged to revel in it. I have to work hard at my protocol every single day; it's not something I can half do or stop because I think I'm doing well.

Thursday, March 1, 2018

Yesterday was a busy day. At one point I sat in my little car and had a very long hard cry because, even at Christmas time, I believed that I would never drive again. Being in my car had always been my happy place. Kay reminded me of how hard I have worked to get here. Another friend commented on how they thought a couple of months ago, because my abilities were so rapidly declining, they were fearful for me. Last night I went out for dinner with a friend. I thought I was ordering a safe dinner, but within a couple hours I felt physically sick. I ended up having that hangover effect. It was a lesson. It severely impacted my sleep.

I am actually looking forward to my testing in April, but sometimes it hits me that the clock is still running. Although I am doing well, I am even more aware of the things that I am still struggling with that may not improve.

Friday, March 2, 2018

Yesterday, I came to Les and Cindy's to start house sitting and enjoyed spending a quiet day reading. I finished reading *The Dancing Dementia Dude*. It was a great read. I felt at times Dallas had a window into my brain, things were so similar. I am happy I am once again enjoying reading and listening to my music. Today I slept well, ended my 24-hour fast and watched the third episode of Regain Your Brain.

Funny thing about dementia, a lot of things don't really matter; what matters is how things make me feel. Anything that gives me a better quality of life is for sure what matters. Today I feel good again so my venture eating out that caused a setback was a lesson to be more careful.

Sunday, March 4, 2018

Today a friend said it's like having me back as I was five years ago. That's a huge testament to how much Dr. Bredesen's Protocol is doing for me. It is not always easy for me to be aware of what is happening; it is delightful to know someone sees the positive changes.

Tuesday, March 6, 2018

I am quite shocked at how quickly I lose a day or several previous hours. It's interesting because I never thought my short-term memory was actually that affected. When so many areas are involved, I'm not always aware of lack of progress. I don't know how much this particular area will improve.

Yesterday I had a conversation with a friend who also has dementia. He pointed out that I am still trying to operate in the no-dementia world and reminded me that I am happiest when I am not trying to fit into that world any longer. Our world is different. Even though many of us are doing really well and accomplishing many things that would even be challenging for the mainstream, we are no longer the mainstream. There is much truth in his words. We try to be part of things that we truly are not comfortable with, trying to hang on to old pieces of self, trying to protect those in our circle from much of our realities. We want to maintain relationships; we work hard to be as normal as possible in spite of our abnormalities.

We also talked about how we all fall prey to convincing ourselves that we're getting better. The reality is, there still is not a cure. I cannot go off course even a little bit because if I do I know all the symptoms will reappear.

Chapter Sixteen

Saturday, March 10, 2018

I have a job! I am working as telephone operator and customer liaison person on Saturdays at a car dealership and learning to substitute for the Monday to Friday woman. Today I have my third day of training. The first day I was so overwhelmed I thought I wouldn't be able to cope. I persevered, did nothing else, got lots of sleep and day two was not so overwhelming. A light dinner and more sleep. I woke up this morning looking forward to today because I am training for my actual position. I know I could not consistently work so many days.

This is a new position within the company. I am blessed by the kindness and understanding shown to me. They had me fill out a paper so they would have it readily available should I have a crisis and they could get me paramedics. I have discussed how my brain functions so my job and duties will be added as I feel able to manage. They have offered me as much training as I feel I need so that I can be successful at my job.

Although I was told by all the various agencies not to tell potential employers about my illness, I have found honesty is the best policy. These people are interested, compassionate, understanding, and more than willing to help. By working only one day a week I hope to manage for a good long time. They are also supportive of my going to the conference in Chicago. I told my sister-in-law last night it feels like this is my reward for working so hard and diligently at finding ways to help myself. Feeling inspired!

Monday, March 12, 2018

My three days of training triggered my fatigue. Yesterday, I could not follow conversations. I was so tired both mentally and physically that I could do nothing. By 7 PM I was running a hot bath full of Epson salts and was in bed by 7:30. Today I didn't wake up until 7 AM. I can still feel the fatigue but it is lifting. I am looking forward to my four-hour day today. Then that's it until Friday when I will do four more then a full day Saturday. After that I should be just doing Saturdays which will be much more manageable for me. I must work hard to keep everything in balance so I don't have a downward slide and more TIAs. I missed my video conversations with my DAI friends last week. They have become such an important part of my life.

Saturday, March 17, 2018

This next weekend we are kicking off our DIA on-line fundraiser, WRAD (World Rocks Against Dementia) to fund speakers to the Conference in Chicago. Please help support those living with dementia. Please help spread the word about this very worthwhile event. I feel empowered these days and I know that 'together we are stronger' is so true.

"If you are not appearing, you are disappearing."– Jan Arden.

Tuesday, March 20, 2018

My short-term memory is really bad right now, probably because I've overdone things lately. My brain decides what is important and the rest is tossed away.

Yesterday was my monthly meeting with the Alzheimer's group. I told them about DAI and hoped one day we could do a special zoom chat.

Saturday evening, I felt a new phenomenon that I don't remember experiencing before. I was out walking Phoebe in a less familiar area and was trying to find my way back to our road when I panicked and felt heavy anxiety to the point of tears. Normally being lost is a great adventure for me. That doesn't seem to be the case anymore. I managed my way through it and learned another lesson: when my brain is fatigued, I can't do certain things and going into unfamiliar areas is one of them.

Wednesday, March 21, 2018

Today I only have one appointment then I will take the rest of the day to free my mind and rest my brain…hmm, that sounds like something out of the sixties…

Yesterday I met with Sherry from the Alzheimer's Society. She totally agrees with me that there are a lot of things that need to be done differently and/or better. She wrote down two pages of notes to take to her regional managers' meeting and she will meet with me in April to let me know how her proposals are accepted. She wasn't aware there was an Alzheimer's Association International Conference in Chicago in July! Yes, that right! She has never heard of the book, *Awakening from Alzheimer's*, she has never heard of DAI. When I told her about our fundraising efforts, she said, "They won't help with that because they like to raise money for their own efforts."

Wait a minute, is this not the organization that is supposed to be helping people with dementia??? I suggested they could help with advertising, etc. She will take it to the meeting but is not hopeful. Wouldn't it be great if the Alzheimer's Society could work with DAI to give people this safe place where they could be understood, and accepted? She agreed, but whether they will, depends on the people in the upper positions of the organization. They should be helping promote people living with the illness to be out there doing speaking engagements and things of that sort, to end the stigmas and to educate people. I told her about my frustrations with the fact they collect so much money on the auspice of helping us, yet very little actually gets down to the people with dementia. The three big pharmaceutical companies pulled their funding for research because they have not found a cure after years and years of trying. Yet Dr. Dale Bredesen and his counterparts are having a major impact; perhaps some funding should go there, where we are seeing good results.

Friday, March 23, 2018

I feel content that I have done my part and worked hard to get the word out about our DAI World Rocks Against Dementia fundraiser today. I am proud of putting myself out there beyond my comfort zone to do it.

I am wishing my two step children and grandchildren were closer so I could spend more time with them. I do understand that I don't have the right to impose myself on them. As much as I appreciate the love of family and friends, they cannot bring the same kind of support that having a partner would have. I think about my husband and how for all his gruffness, whenever I was sick, he was such a gentle and supportive presence. I shall miss him until I meet him again. I'm melancholy today.

Chapter Seventeen

Saturday, March 24, 2018

This morning as I prepare to head off to my first day flying solo on my new job, I have a great peace about me. Our Dementia Alliance International 'World Rocks Against Dementia' was very well received. Off to work I go feeling: if we could pull off this fundraiser in such a short amount of time then I've got this.

Sunday, March 25, 2018

I really enjoyed my day yesterday and my brain didn't let me down. That thought always sits there at the very edge of my mind. This week is going to be a resting week, just relaxing, walking, enjoying whatever sunshine we receive, I need this because my body feels tired, and I know the importance of listening to my body.

Wednesday, March 28, 2018

Yesterday was all 'Out': getting fresh air. My little dog and I walked early in the morning then later in the afternoon we managed to do miles. I didn't have to be anywhere or do anything. In the afternoon, I attended our DAI webinar. It was fantastic! Aside from being mad at myself for not getting my one question spoken with clarity, I took away so much from the webinar, an educational piece everyone working in the health field should have to attend.

I'm realizing, to manage one eight-hour day of paid work, I take about three days to recover. It's worth it because it keeps me engaged, my brain gets to learn new things, I get to feel stimulated and feel like I am contributing.

This illness has taught me things I could never learn from a classroom or textbook. It has taught me about the brain's incredible adaptability, my own adaptability and that of others living with the illness. It has opened my world up to moving in a whole different direction.

I look beyond the norm because the norm no longer applies to me. We should use our voices. In doing so, ideas that were thought to be true get turned inside out. We need people doing original research and looking for new ideas, but more importantly we need those of us living with the illness to question, to challenge what is expected within the known perimeter of our illness, to stand up and show them the illness from the other side. This helps all those people do a better job, which will enrich the lives of all living with an illness that is still largely misunderstood.

We will get slammed. People generally resist change. People don't like to hear that what they are doing could be improved, or worse, could be detrimental. I, like many others, will take the heat. I must say there also comes great learning in the doing. It's hard work, likely the hardest job of my life.

Sunday, April 1, 2018

Today was a great example of how things can become unbearably difficult in moments. I went into my regular grocery store looking for one item. I, suddenly, was standing in the middle of an isle thinking nothing about this makes sense! I could find no pattern in the arrangement of the goods and had no idea how to navigate the aisles to find what I wanted. My sister called me that moment from her home town. I was so close to tears because I couldn't make sense of the store. Chatting with her changed my brain pattern enough I could walk out of the store empty handed. She helped me when my brain couldn't do what I needed it to do. I've shopped for almost 50 years, but today the store was an alien place. No one in that store could see my distress and had no idea of the crisis I was in. Sisters are such blessings!

Wednesday, April 4, 2018

I keep trying not to be tired but it seems everything takes so much out of me now. Although I am tired today, I am happily getting ready for company. My friends, Les and Terri, are arriving on their way home from Arizona; they're only staying for the night but it will be nice to see them. I am hoping to meet all my goals today. We'll see what I actually accomplish, what gets missed or forgotten. I'm keeping things simple, vegetables and marinated meat to cook on my table barbecue, oven roasted vegetables, a couple of salads with cookies and ice cream for dessert. I no longer am so hard on myself for messing things up. I have learned to be kind; after all I do have dementia.

Sunday, April 8, 2018

Years ago I built a presentation for those in the nursing field; due to budget issues it was never actually used. Called 'Unattended Sorrow,' it notes that nurses often sit with someone who is leaving this world. Actually, it was one of my passions because I felt those people have much to share with us. These caregivers often partake in death and loss but are given no support or time to process the toll it takes on them.

I rethought the premise from the standpoint of dementia. We too endure multiple losses, the loss of job, loss of friends and family, loss of life style, loss of abilities, and on and on, but for most there is no support system in place to help with the process. It's another reason why Dementia Alliance International is so important. I wish every person diagnosed would automatically be given the link to this organization. Here is where personal support begins, from peer to peer assistance to webinars with prominent people working in the field. If proper support is in place depression is not so prominent, less medication is needed and a better quality of life emerges.

This last week has been really trying, scary and sad for me, yesterday was a little better, I received support from the most unlikely places.

Tuesday, April 10, 2018

Yesterday I had the pleasure of meeting Carolyn who is launching a new business venture to help those diagnosed with dementia be able to remain independent and at home. Her focus will be on the care giver so I suggested that, in order to better support the care giver, she should talk privately with the one who actually has been diagnosed. The reason I suggested it be private is because so often, once diagnosed, people's partners or care givers start speaking for them.

The biggest change needed is teaching care givers to stop taking over and doing everything. They should be taught how to help their charges do as much as they possibly can. It may not be done the way it once was, as quickly, or to the same standard, but if care givers were taught to accept those limitations the recipient's frustration level would not be so high.

When the care giver takes over tasks and conversations the dementia sufferer can do, he/she reacts by becoming depressed and withdrawn or frustrated and angry. Then he/she is labelled difficult, challenging, or violent. If care givers could learn to accept the person and their new way of managing things, they could help ensure they are set up to thrive. This would create a lot less caregiver burnout. I would also put into their tool box Dementia Alliance International. By providing the person diagnosed and the care giver with that information and giving them the ability to join us weekly on our support group chats, it provides a time for the care person to have that hour 'off,' to regroup, enjoy a cup of tea, whatever they may fancy and the person living with the illness feels more supported. Today I am grateful for those who are willing to learn from us.

Friday, April 13, 2018

I am losing days, not just hours. Talking with my sister-in-law yesterday; she's worried because she's noticed a decline in me the last few weeks. One of the things we talked about is that I might be too busy because my short-term memory is bad. I don't think I'm doing anything and I add more tasks to my day. My dementia brain can't do busy all the time. I laugh about it because it all feels so crazy. I do feel like my whole being is off right now, scattered, disorganized, unable to stay focused. Perhaps in my drive to do something 'normal,' my body is telling me the old normal is no longer a devise that belongs in my tool box.

I had lovely visits yesterday with three different friends. I spend the bulk of my time alone so I do appreciate the times that visits happen. They break the loneliness. I woke up feeling better today.

Sunday, April 15, 2018

I was talking with my dear friend Kate the other day about the fact that, whether we do things or not the fatigue will be there so we have to keep working; if we don't we will drown in our disease. So, the very things that add to our natural fatigue also save us from our disease. Confusing! Some people wonder why I would use so much energy to advocate when fatigue plagues me so much of the time. It is because this is where I find hope for people coming after me, where I can help them have an easier time than I have had.

I don't have the joys others have of planning my retirement, planning a future and if those of us who are willing to stand up and talk about our illness didn't subject ourselves to the fatigue involved to do it, then there will never be a chance for better treatment, better understanding. As one doctor stated, "We don't have time to wait."

Tuesday, April 17, 2018

Today was the appointment with my specialist, Dr. Pretorious. He expected to see me looking much the same as in late November; but he was pleasantly surprised. Instead of testing me he wanted to talk about all the things

I was doing. We started with Dr. Dale Bredesen's Protocol. He was aware of it, he asked how I used it, what types of supplements I took, what kinds of food I eat and stressed the importance of the walking and Pilates/Physio piece of my therapy. He can't officially endorse anything until all the trials are done but he can tell people about the effects it's having on people who are trying the program. He wants me to keep going because by doing all these things I give myself the best life possible. Aricept is of minimal help by itself.

I took him a copy of my speech I will be giving in Chicago. He told me it is more important than I realize because it is the only way things will get better for others. He also said all this will keep me well, beyond anything he can do for me. Few realize how devastating a diagnosis dementia is and most sufferers don't want to do all the things I am doing to have a good life. They want a quick 'feel better' option and he hopes that we can reach more people to show them there is life after diagnosis. He read my paper for the webinar that I will be a panelist on next Wednesday and said it's another valuable piece to help others. Having his support is important and we discussed how it makes it easier for him and Dr. Cunningham to help me when I'm so willing to help myself. My next appointment is in October.

Wednesday, April 18, 2018

I've talked before about unattended sorrow. I think I've been doing a lot of grieving the last few weeks. I will have to do more because losses will continue to happen until the day I die. The grieving is often put aside, pushed down, partly because it takes so much energy just to get through an average day. If we allow ourselves to feel the emotions, reflect, and acknowledge our losses, then we must use up precious energy. But if we listen, our bodies will let us know it's time to let the grief go to gain strength for the next onslaught. These losses will not seem like a big deal to many. In fact, people make jokes about them. When every loss means your life is slipping away a little more. Piece by piece, it does become a big deal.

Saturday, May 12, 2018

Yesterday I got myself an Alexa (a virtual assistant developed by Amazon) so she will now be my home assistant. I will be setting her up on Monday. I am constantly late; I completely forget what day it is. I hope this little piece of technology will take away the frustration I feel when I mix things up.

A younger and younger population is now living with dementia. We want to be able to live well with our illness and not be cast aside by society. We can change things and make things better for people if the 'powers that be' get rid of their egos and actually do business with us. What we need is some common sense all across the board. I'm feeling the frustration after a week of trying to help others navigate the diagnosis process.

Sunday, May 13, 2018

Today has been glorious, then utterly horrid. It started out brilliantly with my homemade medicine getting my little Phoebe up and raring to go this morning. Bouncy and happy, boy did she want to walk, about 1.5 hours' worth.

Then I was trying to get my chaos organized; housework has become a huge challenge and I get so mad at myself. I've always prided myself on my house being neat and tidy. Just the challenge of remembering where things go, unbelievably frustrating. After a number of hours and some tears I struggled through that.

Another burst of happiness; my little dog brought her toys out to play; it melted my heart to see her having such a good day. She's been mostly sleeping lately and not wanting to walk a lot.

Finally, I decided to try to set up Alexa; it's supposed to make my life easier right? The instructions seemed simple enough, I thought this should be okay...the joke was on me. I tried many times to follow the instructions, getting the app going, needing this password and that password and secondary something or others. I ended up so angry I had one of those silent screams that are so loud no one else can hear them. I cried a big cry after realizing how far down the ladder my abilities have slipped. Yes, there are people who will help me with this little device, but somehow, I still find it necessary to try. I eventually set up the basics but I know the device can do more.

Book Four
Successes

Chapter Eighteen

Monday, June 25, 2018

Something is changing, not liking the feeling, balance off again, thought process a mess, time to get hard core on Bredesen Protocol. Sometimes I wonder how long to keep fighting; what am I actually fighting for? Flat effect. Not happy, not sad, not anything, just am. I know this will pass whenever this change completes and resettles. Sometimes I want to cry, I want to scream and rage, but I don't, no point. Living alone means there's never anyone around to help me through those darkest moments. Sometimes staring down this road of being on my own, I ask myself why fight anymore? In one month, I will be in Chicago giving, likely, the most important speech of my life, maybe the last one. Something in me feels so strong, a change is happening but I can't explain it.

I started the Bredesen Protocol after joining Dementia Alliance International, and finding the DAI Brain Health Hub. I started reading Dr. Dale Bredesen's book The End of Alzheimer's. The book helped put me on a path to living well with my illness. The Protocol is based on feeding our brains lots of healthy fats, bulletproof coffee, medium chain triglycerides or MCT oils, butter, blended with coffee, delicious. I use supplements, magnesium, B12. My diet follows the keto style, but with specifics that help reduce inflammation in my brain. The Protocol has helped way beyond what I had hoped for.

Friday, June 29, 2018

I have not been well this last while, my doctor has been away, I went to the walk-in clinic earlier in the week, one doctor did her best to be helpful and supportive. Yesterday went back to the walk-in clinic, was told by another doctor that I shouldn't come back, they don't have access to all my medical records, I have the best doctor in town, I should just go upstairs and tell them to get me in to see my own doctor.

I explained my doctor wasn't there and I needed help now. He went on and on about how he would first have to look at all of my scans and the CT's of my brain, so there's nothing he can do for me at a walk-in clinic. I tried to explain that I needed help dealing with an infection, not my brain. I was going from being feverish to having chills, I had a rash on both my cheeks, I wanted treatment for an infection, dangerous to me if left untreated. I was dismissed, left in tears, felt totally abandoned by our medical system. It felt like he was saying, "well you have dementia so there's no point in helping you."

I am enraged by this! Walk-in clinics are supposed to be for when our doctors are unavailable so that we don't clog up the Emergency Room. I did go upstairs to my doctor's office and talked to the girls. My doctor will be back today so I will see him later this morning. People believe Canada has the best medical system; it is until it becomes a necessary part of your life that you have to continually navigate.

(Later) The difference a compassionate doctor can make. Infection addressed, specialists called asking to move me up as an urgent case, blood work all done, a new plan in place, an apology for what transpired, an acknowledgment that he felt partly responsible for not foreseeing that something like this could happen.

He smiled and said, "You've got a lot of unique challenges so not everyone will know where to start." His office has full instructions that if I 'walk in' or call, I am seen. If he is not there, someone else will see me; they will all have his permission to call him. If the office is not open, then I bypass the walk-in and go to the ER where my full chart is available: with his permission to call if needed.

Now loaded up on antibiotics and a few changes in other meds; using great care to try not to worsen the dementia side effects until I get an appointment with the specialist. No CPAP machine either, he doesn't want the extra air pressure on my head, I'm to sleep propped up for a bit as well. He said some people require special care and to be seen; I am that person. Felt totally understood and heard and supported today.

Tuesday, July 3, 2018

Haven't written for a bit, haven't been able to paint for a few days or read. I have not been feeling well; I look extremely fatigued but have been sleeping a lot. My doctor called today while I was enjoying a visit with Karen (the physiotherapist). She stopped by because I haven't been feeling up to being out and about. He thinks I started with a TIA then this infection which created a huge accumulation of events that magnified my dementia related issues. Today we are going to stop some more medications to see if they are interacting incorrectly. I am wondering if following the protocol has caused so many changes in my body that it changed how the meds were working. We'll stop certain ones for four days then re-evaluate until we see which need to be changed or stopped altogether. We won't mess with my Aricept. Hopefully I will start feeling better.

It was decided I would stop two of my meds, first the Statin. Research has shown Statin, one of the most widely prescribed heart medications, is of no value to women and has very little positive effects for men. It only helps those who have had a previous heart attack or stroke and then the help is minimal. There is mounting concern; my specialist told me he doesn't understand why it is still being used.

The other medication was Ramapril, which was causing side effects as well: dizziness, fatigue. It always felt to me like it exaggerated my dementia symptoms. There was a noticeable difference for me and the meds have not been restarted. It is my wish to stick with natural treatments as much as possible.

It's amazing how one small disturbance in my health can worsen a large section of dementia symptoms. Then I have to ride out the storm hoping that everything settles and doesn't drop me another step down in the dementia scale. These adjustments are always scary; they are a reminder of how precious every good day is.

Friday, July 6, 2018

Ginger and coconut oil, this will be my bed time drink for the foreseeable future. This disease is so cruel, it tears you apart, steals pieces you can feel slipping away, a landslide you can't stop. Then it sits, plays nice for a while, until you're lulled into almost believing it isn't real. Abruptly it grabs you, throws you up against the wall and reminds you that Mr. Dementia is still in full control.

Yet we find laughter, we find tools to help ourselves because no one else is doing it for us. We are doing it with our protocols, with being on top of the newest, most up to date information available. We educate ourselves; we collectively have a better working knowledge than our doctors. Do you know, most doctors and specialists receive on average 12 hours training on dementia? I remember, when I was nursing, being so disgusted that nurses/care aids received so little useful education on dementia or end of life care. No wonder people with dementia are often treated with barely concealed distaste.

Saturday, July 7, 2018

Enjoying morning coffee on my pretty little deck before going to my Saturday job; feeling so unbelievably grateful that they have been so supportive by giving me time off as required, depending on what's happening with my dementia. I'm truly blessed that they have shown such understanding.

Spent a great deal of time trying to figure out what was necessary so I could work today; got up at 5 this morning to ensure I would be there by 9. People talk about needing balance in life; for people living with dementia it is an absolute necessity. Balance, for us, is reserving our energy and brain power and choosing carefully where to focus it. This need is something that is difficult for people to understand.

Today I will be happy that I have rebounded enough to return to my job, understanding full well that it is not likely to be sustainable for a very long period, but today I will just be grateful.

I am no longer able to keep track of when people are on shift. I used to remember all those things; always knew in my head when friends were working. Now I wake up every morning wondering. I was, at one point, trying to devise ways to manage those kinds of things because, after being told, by the next day I had forgotten again. It became too stressful to try to manage the unmanageable.

Sunday, July 8, 2018

Laughing at myself tonight, I have a variety of appointments this week, but my notes on my Alexa are reminders of something happening at a certain time but no notation of what it might be. I guess I'll be making phone calls in the morning trying to connect all the dots…

Tuesday, July 10, 2018

Yesterday turned into an interesting day. Figuring out one appointment led to the realization I had a two-hour meeting in the afternoon and confirmed two appointments for today, one for tomorrow and one for Thursday.

I saw my doctor yesterday; I am to reinstate my CPAP machine, use oxygen as required at night, stay off the two meds, my infection cleared up. He was most impressed how all the different tests showed such remarkably normal levels. Cholesterol is perfect! I am to keep on my Protocol; it's having a good effect.

Yesterday, I also took part in an action planning meeting with the local Interior Health board, to identify holes in the system and help put actions in place to fill them. Describing my recent experiences triggered a look at a new program designed to help when needed from diagnosis onward. There it was, exactly what I had explained, most of those services I am excluded from because I have dementia. Everyone there had difficulty believing that until seeing it in black and white, glaring at them off the page, 'not available for anyone with DEMENTIA.'

I can tell you, today there will be meetings about this, and I am to call tomorrow to receive some answers as to why and what they are going to do about it. (Nothing was ever done. I have resigned out of frustration.) I am fortunate because of the doctor I have. What about all the people who don't have a Dr. Cunningham? Those are the people I really worry about.

Thanks to those who checked in with me while I was not managing very well; it was appreciated.

Wednesday, July 11, 2018

I went to Kalamalka Lake this morning for a swim. I was the only one in the shoulder deep water looking back at the beach and watching various groups interacting. In that moment, I wondered how many of them truly realized how fortunate they were to have family and friends; I venture to guess most take it for granted. It also made me aware of how much has changed for me: how many losses have taken place in the last couple of years but mostly in the last six months. I feel it, it stings, I feel the tears rise to the surface. I swallow, tell myself it's okay, I know I don't fit in the 'mainstream' anymore and I no longer try. My life is challenging enough.

On the other hand, my dementia family is growing. (If you think about it, that is actually a sad thing because it means another person has started the journey.) There is where I am accepted every day in whatever muddled way I am present. There is no expectation, no judgment, only kindness, support, understanding and love. Oh, and laughter. Laughter that causes you to have tears run down your face, belly laughs that are good for the soul. Some have impressive backgrounds, interesting lives and careers, but everyone is equal because everyone is fighting the same battle.

In a strange way, I feel privileged to be part of this group, to live with this illness to experience something the rest of the world lacks. (Boy, who ever thought those words would go hand in hand with dementia?) One side of the spectrum is this joy and happiness despite living with a terminal illness, on the other side a sadness that most of us have to experience and accept: the loss of so many people from our lives.

Saturday, July 14, 2018

Yesterday was the final turning point on the road to another good stretch. My brain fog is gone, my energy is back and I can think clearly.

Raising money for Chicago was a daunting task. Some amazing friends helped by donating to and hosting a garage sale and a hotdog sale. Others contributed by buying my paintings, selling my clear glass sand potted succulent plants in their stores, and donating directly to Dementia Alliance International. We were able to cover airfare, hotels, meals and transportation.

Tuesday, July 17, 2018

One week today I leave for Chicago; the days are flying by. I am as prepared as I can be, I've done the best I can with the speeches; I'm still trying to organize everything else I have to do this week. Dr. Cunningham called yesterday. I have a follow up appointment with him August 9th so he will be seeing how I am post trip.

Chicago here I come…but I was terrified of public speaking. I have done very limited amounts of it, usually in small groups, usually in front of people I am familiar with. I was so far out of my comfort zone. With my friend June Millius in tow to help me navigate Chicago and get to where I need to be when I need to be there, we left Kelowna via Air Canada through Vancouver.

The flight was easy, getting to the hotel by train was easier. Chicago was warm and welcoming. I found it simply lovely to walk the streets late in the evening without feeling uneasy. Trains, buses, water taxis and a week pass made it simple to get around.

Signing in day: Finding McCormick Place the next morning was easier than expected. I was beyond excited to meet the other members of Dementia Alliance International, my friends and colleagues. We all worked so hard to get here. This will be our time to shine, to have our voices heard on an International stage for all those now living with dementia, for all those coming behind us. Even amidst the excitement of meeting in person for the first time, we never lost sight of our reason for being here and what we hoped to accomplish

And there was Maria, we were so excited to see each other I can't describe how it felt but our hugs and squeals said it all, emotions were running so high. Then Kate, then Mike, then John, then Jerry; later it would be Tetsuro and Tomo, and Kazuka. So much happiness! We were all just so glad to be able to be together it didn't matter who forgot what or when, we laughed till we cried then laughed some more. Pure joy.

That evening was the first meeting with the people in the print/press room to tell us when and where to be the next day. Then off to meet the tech guys. This is a big production, this is a conference on a scale I had not attended before. I likened it to a movie set: quiet rooms, people assigned to help with anything needed, the tech guys simply amazing. Back to the hotel. I was exhausted yet emotionally charged, content, thankful to have June with me. She was a calming presence, always close by to ensure she could help me remember where and what came next. Friends who are willing to give up time and energy to help us live our best life with dementia are priceless and June is a gem. Late that night, 3 AM actually, I woke up and made changes to my speech. Okay, day one and I had survived.

Second day, Day One of the Conference: first thing in the morning off to the print room to get changes made. The tech guys needed me in early, the room was closed off, no access to anyone else except me, sound checks done, lighting checked, microphones set up at the right level for me. They did a run through so I knew exactly how it would go, how they would introduce me, then they gave me the gift of time to sit quietly, clear my mind, go to that still place where everything is peaceful, until it was time to open the doors. I should have been trembling with fright, but from somewhere outside of me this sense of calm and peace engulfed me, I don't think I have ever experienced that before.

I was introduced, took my place at the podium and released my thoughts. I don't actually remember what I said. I learned later I received a standing ovation. I have finally listened to my speech which has been released on Dementia Alliance International You Tube Channel, as well as Twitter, Facebook, and Dementia Alliance International Web Page. My words held more impact than I thought I could deliver. They came across very real, with the level of emotion I wanted.

As soon as the other speeches in that introductory portion were finished, I was bombarded by people who wanted to talk to me, to connect with me, again something I had never experienced. The closest thing I could liken it to was movie stars being chased by paparazzi! I knew I had accomplished what I had come to Chicago to do, to be heard, to be strong enough in voice that people actually listened. Now all I wanted to do was run to my Dementia Alliance International family and decompress.

We had more people, including myself, who would be speaking in the next few days and we all needed to support each other. Something magical happened with us, everyone spoke so well, every speech was incredibly touching. Our words had a huge impact on all those in attendance. Dementia Alliance International reached a new level. Already a world-renowned organization thanks to people like Kate Swaffer, we were officially recognized at this conference. I believe we cannot be ignored any longer.

Chapter Nineteen

Saturday, July 28, 2018

I believe all the hard work that those ahead of us in Dementia Alliance International have done was culminated in yesterday's speeches. I am honored to stand with so many amazing people. During the question and answer session of the panel discussion, for me, the moment that stood out was when Kate's husband Peter, warned everyone in that room:

"Change is coming, these people aren't going away, they are getting stronger and louder, you need to listen, you need to start helping make the changes happen, because your organizations are not going to survive if you don't get on board, you need to support them in their efforts."

His words touched me deep in my heart because it was exactly what I was feeling, the momentum, the power of everyone who stood up and used their voices. The president of Alzheimer's USA came to me and told me "no matter what, you need to keep using your voice." People were there from Belgium, Pakistan, India, so many countries, and I realized at that moment I was right where I was meant to be, being part of something truly incredible.

DAI members are changing the face of dementia. It may take a long time before it trickles down to communities like mine but it isn't about me, it's too late for me, I've felt the stigma, fought the medical system. It's for everyone else following me; knowing I am giving a huge piece of myself to help others not experience those things has me feeling a sense of pride.

I eventually got to meet the man from Scotland who had tweeted about my standing ovation. He said my speech brought him to tears; he even teared up talking to me about how it impacted him. I don't remember people clapping; all I remember is looking down at all my DAI family and seeing nothing but love. I had told them I would try to do them and DAI proud and I felt content knowing I had an impact at levels I never thought possible.

Sunday, July 29. 2018

Excited for another day; can't believe we will have to start saying our goodbyes. We all had a great dinner together last night, and over today and tomorrow we will start saying 'until next time.' It appears next time for Jerry Wylie and me will be when we speak in Jamaica in December 2019. We both feel very honored.

I have always said DAI has changed my life but coming here and meeting everyone is life altering. I have been inundated by people wanting to connect to work together on various projects. It will take some time to process everything. This morning, as I got ready, I felt as though the answer to the question, 'Why do I have dementia?' had been answered: it brought me my purpose. I was not striving in a positive environment during my working years, but here, in this organization, I can feel the impact we are making.

I had a great dinner with Mike and Cheryl, John and Cindy, Pete and June. After, June and I took a boat ride on the canal then a walk through this spectacular city along the river front. Also, I learned that last night I became Oma to a beautiful little boy, Easton Benjamin. I am exhausted, teary, but proud.

Monday, July 30, 2018

My last day in Chicago, such a beautiful city, clean, safe, friendly. Their hospitality and kindness did not go unnoticed. Interestingly even though there are over 3 million people living here it never felt as though I was in a crowded noisy city; they have done a tremendous job with their city planning.

Waking up this morning I felt content but sad; it may be the first and last time I see some of these people face to face. A huge thank you to June for doing such a great job of keeping me on time, taking care of all my belongings and making sure I was going in the right direction as I ran from session to session. We have had some great laughs, and I could not have managed all this without her.

Wednesday, August 1, 2018

I woke up many times last night, totally disoriented, trying to figure out where I was, what I was doing, thoughts and words all jumbled together. This is the toll paid for advocating and pushing myself. I am still sitting in bed having my bulletproof coffee, my little dog content just to lay beside me. I'll take her for a walk today but will not press myself too much.

I have to spend some time putting some thoughts to paper; I only have today as a rest day. I work for three consecutive days covering for some people who are away. I am not sure how that will turn out but I am going to try because they have done so much for me.

Thursday, August 2, 2018

Last night I woke with my heart racing, panicked, disoriented. Sitting up in my bed I could not figure out why I was in it, why I had chosen to be there, it didn't feel familiar. Eventually I got out of bed, walked into the other room, looked out over the balcony, walked back into my room and was delighted to get into my own bed! I hate the pieces and parts of this disease that create such distress.

Yesterday, talking with my sister-in-law, I was trying to describe being in Chicago with my DAI family. I had such a sense of calm, of peace there, and I realize it was because, with them, I didn't have to work so hard to normalize myself. I think most of us with dementia expend so much energy every day trying not to make mistakes with our words and actions, to make it less frustrating for so called normal people. All that hard work takes extra concentration and causes its own type of stress.

With my DAI family I was at ease, I was comfortable, it truly was what being with family should be. I never needed to apologize for missteps and blunders, laughter and tears flowed freely, complete acceptance allowed me to just be me as I am today instead of trying so hard to be the person that is no longer there. I like this version of me, fun, happy, full of life.

June told me when we were coming home, the reason she wanted to go was because she didn't understand what was happening to me, she wanted to know how to be better able to help me as time goes on. She said she had no idea and understands so much more now. To have someone be so willing to take time out of their own life, away from their own family and do that for me is beyond words. We need a world full of Junes so that we can thrive. She met my DAI family to engage, learn and understand them. She was able to share much of the laughter and tears and came away with a new group of friends. I am forever grateful.

Saturday, August 11, 2018

It's time: time to tell the story of another beginning. For months our DAI group has been talking about the different kind of challenges people who are on their own face. This brought up many issues: one being, why does society make us feel we should no longer attempt to have personal relationships? This is so wrong on so many levels. When you know that a person with dementia may forget a lot of things but the one thing that always remains is feelings, why shouldn't someone with dementia have the same opportunity as everyone else to love and be loved?

So began my incredible journey onto a dating site. My profile had to be real, it had to be honest, it had to ask if someone with a terminal illness could find love or were we destined to be alone forever.

I have been alone for thirteen years. I am worthy, I am capable and I am enough just as I am. I have taken the power out of my dementia, it is part of my daily life, but instead of being depressed and angry about it, I have befriended it. It has given me a purpose I never had before, it has taught me about acceptance, it has taught me that there are silver linings. It has given me a family of friends that enhance the very being of who I am. My dementia and I have learned to love each other, to walk together and dance the Dementia Dance of Life. So here is the profile write up that went on my site, testing, testing, testing.

"I am a 59-year-old woman who loves life. I have a terminal illness; however, I am determined to get at least another ten years of good living. I enjoy road trips, I like exploring new highways and byways, I walk every day. I advocate for myself and others so that we can live our best lives despite our illness. I have more good days but occasionally have some bad ones. I am looking for that person who can laugh with me, create great memories from the simplicity of morning coffee and is able to hold my hand through the hard days. I am not looking for someone to be my care giver; I am looking for a partner to share all that life has to offer. I am kind, positive, love humor, early mornings, campfires. I am not interested in flings, don't like nor do I have time for drama or games, seriously looking for someone to share life's journey with."

I received a lot of nice messages, but not messages about possibilities of meeting. Then a different type of message came through. It resonates deep within me, I look at this person's profile, I wonder if this man is real. Something told me I needed to respond; I did. That led to long conversations, changed to daily video chats as we got to know each other.

Fears crept in, uncertainties, yet they melted away quickly. Our relationship kept growing. I told no one; I wanted no outside opinions on whether it was right or wrong. I wanted it to be what it wanted to be without the outside world interfering.

When we met face to face, it was like coming home; we never skipped a beat. He doesn't live here so what now? Put it out to God and don't stand in the way or try to control the outcome. I was on the first part of a getaway last week when my landlord called to say they have decided to sell my apartment. I should be stressed; I should be anxious. Instead I am calm, peaceful; I know everything will be okay.

Back home, after going up Canoe Mountain to my husband's memorial stone then spending a couple of lovely days with Jim (now you know his name), I came home and met with my landlord. I will be moving out at the end of September; knowing we want to be together we look at how that might work. His first thoughts are making sure it's best for me.

We have a couple of possibilities, we are letting God decide the where, we already know the when. I am now officially with a man who keeps telling me he's not perfect, but he's perfect for me. I know he is not afraid to walk my journey with me, and I with him, (he too has health problems). Every single day we have to enjoy life together is worth taking all the risks. Our children have been told, family has been told. We both have a very clear understanding of how precious time is. If we have the chance to love and be loved, grab it, don't wait, don't hesitate, don't miss a moment of it, together in all of our imperfections we become stronger, we complement each other.

I have finally met someone I feel safe handing my heart to. Yes, there is hope, there are blessings in the tragedy of our illnesses. There is much life for us to breathe in yet, bad days, hard times. Challenges will be softened by the gentleness of having someone by my side. Getting ready to move begins. Happiness, love, companionship, being best friends to each other begins. I can do all my advocating work from anywhere as long as I have my computer. Phoebe, my dog, loves him too and is excited to have him.

I met Warren and Cara through my niece Tara. Cara had helped with a garage sale when I was selling my little yellow house. Fast forward a couple of years: I am in search of a spot to rent. Cara hears and immediately contacts me, they have purchased a condo, have almost completed renovations and would love to have me for their tenant. I went and viewed the property with Cara, it was perfect, it looked out onto green space, with lots of trees, birds, ducks, deer, a lovely little creek running behind it. I moved in hoping it was going to be my long-term place. I loved it there, perfect size (2 bedroom), the perfect neighborhood, easy walking to doctors, grocery etc. My little dog and I were content there.

I loved all my neighbors, one in particular Garret a young fellow, kind, funny and always checking to see if I needed anything and if he could help me in any way. He helped when I was struggling with getting my Alexa set up, I stay in touch with him today. Just shy of a year of being there, Warren and Cara had to come to some difficult decisions and one of them caused a devastating blow to me. They had to sell the apartment. When they informed me, I put on my brave face, said I understood and for them not to feel bad.

I then made decisions based on the fact that I no longer had a place to live, that I probably would not have made if my housing had been secure.

Tuesday, August 14, 2018

People always wonder why I am up so early. This is the time of day my brain is at its best, it's done restoring and cleaning out all those old information files, it's at its optimal performance level. The world is quiet; there is not all the noise of daily life bombarding my brain. I normally write in the morning, work on anything that takes thought, try to book any important appointments. I embrace these hours, they are free of so much of the struggles I endure later in the day, I grab and enjoy them.

I have not attended any large group gatherings for a long time because there is too much noise happening around me which disorients me; I know the things to avoid so as not to end up sick. However, I am facing a crossroads which creates an element of stress.

Jim's daughter is getting married; it's a large event. I want to attend with him in a manner that is the least harmful to my wellbeing. I won't be able to be there late. We will have discussions on how to plan this so that it works for me and doesn't intrude on his time to enjoy his daughter's day.

I have a lot of things happening right now which I am wading through with great care so as not to send my body reeling. The importance of our partner's willingness to learn, understand and help set us up for success in daily challenges is imperative. As I move from the realm of living alone with dementia to living with a partner, there will be much for him to understand. I'm grateful that my DAI family will be there to help us as we navigate these uncharted waters. I am blessed to have met someone who is willing to take my hand and face my problems with me.

Sunday, August 19, 2018

2:18 AM, it's one of those up and down kind of nights, no point fighting it. My brain wants to replay many pieces of my life like a Greek tragedy. I wake with my heart racing, tears streaming down my face. Those events that made me strong also remind me that I am human, I feel, I fear. Many that replay in vivid color, with such emotion, drain me.

One of the events that haunt my dreams occurred in 2009. Part of my brain keeps searching for what happened to me; it's like it wants to unlock the mystery but can't. My doctors say my body has built-in mechanisms that protect me during very traumatic events. I will likely never regain the memory that left me looking like someone had taken a baseball bat to my head: whole head swollen and black and blue, a severe concussion and no memory of what happened. The last I remember is going to bed. I sometimes wonder if this was the tipping point into dementia.

Yet, at the very core of my being I feel calm, I feel an incredibly beautiful peace. It is from this place that I find my ability to be positive in spite of, to thrive in spite of, to move forward without hesitation, I overcome, I find contentment, I find happiness.

(Next day) By early afternoon everything crashed, vision, balance, coordination. I was disoriented; going to bed was the only thing I could do. After lying down for a couple of hours, I was slightly better. I managed, by being extra careful so I didn't fall, to feed myself, tidy up the place and get ready for bed. My routines are off because of the heavy smoke in the air from forest fires; I am not keeping up with my walking.

Wednesday, August 21, 2018

This morning my brain is in pain. It always astonishes me at how quickly this disease can take a great day and turn it upside down. It's like living life on a tight rope and trying to keep everything balanced. Even when I am thriving, I am monitoring myself, keeping my finger on the pulse so to speak, watching and paying attention for any of the indicators that the dementia demons are coming out to play. Most days my strength and resolve carry and manage it well, but every once in a while, it makes me just want to sit and cry. Time to get up and push through.

Wednesday, August 22, 2018

The fog has dissipated. I think the thinning of the smoke in the air has helped. I have such inner peace, a calm right in the deepest depths of the core of me which gets me through the rough days. I don't 'what if,' I take what is before me, embrace it, and truly live for today and all that it offers

.

Chapter Twenty

Friday, August 24, 2018

During the times one of our dementia family members struggles with challenges or when they have to watch a loved one cope with life's problems: if the world could see, they would observe people from around the globe stand together to offer support. They wrap those in need in a cloak of love and protection, understanding the special challenges. No one judges if the person is making the right or wrong choice, everyone helps them with whatever choice they make. We 'get it.'

This speaks volumes about the very special organization that Dementia Alliance International is. Language /country/ time differences are no barriers; we are all intimately connected. Some days it takes us all standing together to carry the worry and pain. Today we pray for all of our warriors who are so bravely fighting challenges over and above their normal ones.

Monday, August 27, 2018

I haven't written much lately. We have all been deeply saddened by one of our DAI members unexpectedly losing her spouse. Several other members struggle with serious health issues. My focus has been with them. But there has also been a major change with me; I am amazed I have not had too many health setbacks while making this very fast transition.

I met a lovely man. When we saw each other, we immediately knew we wanted to be together; I felt God had arranged our meeting even though we lived hundreds of miles from each other. I had to move from my apartment by October first, Jim was going to move my direction, we would live in his fifth wheel and figure out the rest from there.

Then he had a health crisis (which is all managed now), got a job opportunity which would start in a week. From Tuesday to Friday we had to hit the gas pedal. I was house sitting thirty kilometers out of town and packing up my apartment at the same time. By Friday evening my place was empty:

everything sold or given away except for personal effects and a few kitchen appliances.

Saturday, after work, I officially departed from Vernon, Jim travelled from Prince George, we met in Kamloops. We will be staying there in the fifth wheel until Sunday then we head off to a new location for his work for the next three months. Beyond that we don't know, except that Vernon will be our home base to maintain doctors, appointments, etc.

Dr. Cunningham says this is what I should be doing, living life, enjoying things while I can. Guess what? Some people said, "You don't know each other well enough!" Some others came up with a whole list of negative what ifs. I say, "What if it's the greatest thing, what if we get to enjoy and appreciate every day together for years, what if we're happy?"

If there is one thing those of us living with dementia understand, it is how very precious each day is. We walk the tight rope daily, but we walk, we don't sit and ponder the what ifs, we are too busy figuring out how to make every minute count. Time is not on our side so we make the most of it.

We knew with 100% certainty that being able to be together was the most important thing, didn't matter where, only that the time was now. We spent yesterday getting ourselves set up, organized. My brain was tired, couldn't find my words, kept forgetting which part I was working on, forgetting what I was saying. But we put in a good day; we worked together as though we've been doing it for years.

Thursday, August 30, 2018

Yesterday, here in Kamloops, I was thankful for my friend, Wendy, who rode shot gun for me. I am actually still smiling at a day that should have had me in tears. The only tears we had were tears of laughter!

The day went like this. I needed to go to the bank but couldn't figure out how to get my bank card to work. I decided to go into the bank and try a teller. Standing in line I saw Wendy's mom, I gave her a hug, she asked, "What are you doing here?"

I said, "I have no idea but I'm going to go see Wendy." Back out the door I go.

This concerned Wendy's mom; she called her. I went to my car then thought, 'I need to go to the bank,' got out of the car, went into the building, stood in line only to learn I was at an auto insurance place not the bank.

Forget this! I went to Tim Hortons and bought Wendy and me a coffee then arrived at her door. She said, "Mom called; she was worried about you." Laughter. I said, "Call and tell her I'm as okay as I can be today."

I had to buy a propane tank. With Wendy in tow, off we went. Within minutes I had forgotten where I was going. Wendy, being a great back up brain, directed me to Costco. No propane tanks available. Left Costco, forgot where I was going. We chatted, we laughed at the fact that here we are, no makeup, hair a mess, just enjoying our time together. A short while ago we would have never ventured out without full makeup and jewelry. Now it was more important to just be together.

It took all day, but by 4 o'clock, the banking was accomplished, the propane tank purchased, and most importantly a glorious yet ridiculous fun day was shared with a wonderful friend who never misses a beat on my bad days. I know this fog comes from the load I have been under, it's taken a lot of brain juice, it's time to slow it all down and let my brain rest a little. Come Sunday, Jim and I will be settled in Spence's Bridge for three months. I will have lots of time to work on my advocating, get back into my routines.

Tuesday, September 4, 2018

Yesterday was spent curled up on the couch, drinking tea, and in bed early. The down days of dementia are frustrating, create anxiety, I find I get so upset with myself as though I somehow should be able to control my brain better. This morning I am suffering what I call 'the hangover effect.' That was Jim's first experience with one of my bad days; he was worried but managed to help me work through it by being very supportive and caring. I am truly blessed that he is so willing to learn the ups and downs about this illness.

Sundowning is very real for many people with dementia. Most people believe that sundowning means aggressive behavior problems but it is actually so much more. It starts when our brain power gets low, usually in the afternoons or early evening. We have used much more brain energy to do the things others do with little thought. Our brains become depleted/fatigued, we can't manage as well, our thoughts become more confused, our words are harder to find, we become physically tired, full of anxiety, frustrated. We want to be able to manage better.

For me the effects of sundowning are very noticeable. I know the signs; I have to modify my expectations at those times to minimize the effects. It's not always easy, I push myself, I forget about the importance of self-care. For me having a partner after so many years on my own, it's now about learning to allow someone else to help me, to care for me. It is going to take me time to accept the fact that I no longer have to manage all on my own.

Yesterday was a really bad day, one I have staved off for quite a while. Being so busy for the last month, it is no surprise that the inevitable happened.

Today I will pace myself as we make our trek to our new location in Spences Bridge. It's only a few hours away but by the time we finish getting hooked up to the pickup here, get there and set up again it will make for a long day. I am hoping to be able to do a lot of work in rural communities and, hopefully, get some of them set up with DAI and the resources that they otherwise do not have access to. So much to look forward to.

Saturday, September 8, 2018

Realizations...I have had many changes in my life in the last while and new things have come to light. One is that the fight/flight (get aggressive or run away) part of my brain is over-active. I think this will lessen as I find myself better rested and managing my new life. I see changes in myself that I would not have necessarily noticed while spending most of my time alone. I am struggling somewhat to navigate through them. It's the part of this disease that I hate, the part where we see the actions that we want to modify but have little control to change things. I do believe, with enough effort to teach my brain new tricks and devising new tools, these newly discovered traits can be managed. Frustrating for sure, but it's just another aspect of living well with my dementia.

It is now very apparent that I repeat myself. I notice it in my videos and in everyday conversations; I hate it! My brain gets stuck and doesn't have the ability to turn off until it feels satisfied. I can't control it, I have to find a way to manage it. Also, my brain is in high gear wanting me to fix things, finish things, say things, do things, so it's driving me crazy. Time to do the hard work and figure out the tricks and tools to change the pathway of my brain: more rewiring required.

I am so very grateful I have a partner who is understanding, kind and patient, but if my actions distress me, I can only imagine what it must be like for him. I don't want to cause him distress if there is any possibility than I can somehow retrain my brain to minimize my troublesome behavior. I have every reason to fight the dementia with everything I have in me now; I have someone who brings so much to my life. I owe us that much: to fight for every good day, every good year we can manage.

I have been given something special in Jim, so I am grateful my disease is slow moving. We can have our time together. It also means I have to do the work to stay as well as possible because I want every moment. It's hard for me to admit there are changes when I see them, don't know how to navigate them, but I am determined...

Sunday, September 9, 2018

This is World Alzheimer's Month; I am using my voice again. While working in dementia care, I watched facility care in Vernon go from creating more personalized spaces and activities for people with dementia, to everything reverting back to a clinical environment. People now have little outdoor time and are medicated with Ativan and various other medicines at the drop of a hat. Management says it's for the persons own good, but I think it is to be able to manage maximum people with minimum staff. I feel it is abusive and neglectful.

Those that rule say it's about money, there isn't enough of it. In my years on the floor, I saw too much money spent on things that had little or no impact on the clients. Rehabilitation and recreation components have been cut to the core and more money spent on making things easier for the managers by having the staff record every minute of their time so no personal hands-on visits to clients have to be made. When they do visit, they check the money, not the level of care.

When I talk about funds that could be better used in nursing homes, I mean that in each budget there are built-in amounts that have to be used by a certain date or it is lost forever. One example: we were told at one time there was $40,000 that needed to be used by our locked Dementia Unit before year's end. The nursing staff wanted it used for programs to benefit the residents. We were told management would use it to create a bigger nursing station.

It's also so frustrating that individuals and families give money that they want specifically used for the residents. I don't believe that purchasing new dishes fit the criteria. That kind of money should be used for activities, outings and creating the ability for all residents to move freely indoors and outdoors. More money should be spent on rehabilitation and a big part of that should be indoor and outdoor activities that catch the interest of the residents.

Dementia clients still have lots to offer. Those in charge say, "They are so aggressive; they behave so badly." Maybe with a more understanding attitude those behaviors would diminish; it's amazing what happens when people are actually treated like important human beings. Even when clients can no longer communicate, they still feel, they still understand when their comfort is not important to their caregivers.

It's time clients have more voice in every aspect of their care. Why are they not speaking to all health care workers, from doctors to kitchen staff, to help them better understand their needs? Why is there not a PWD (Person with Dementia) as part of every rec/rehab department to help implement activities that may actually bring some quality to the life of those living in these environments?

There are many of us around the globe who are demanding our human rights be acknowledged: that we be given the same treatment as those living with various other types of illness. As part of Dementia Alliance International, I am proud to use my voice whenever and however I can to help make change happen.

Tuesday, September 11, 2018

Love is about bringing out the best in each other, it's about caring for one another as much as ourselves, it's about facing the hard stuff together, it's about enjoying the simplicity of all the little things we share. Jim and I are each other's silver linings. Now neither of us have to walk through the final chapter alone. I had given up; I believed I had to spend my last years alone.

The transition has been flawless; it was meant to be. Sometimes life greatest tragedies bring about the greatest rewards; this is one of those instances. I am one lucky and blessed girl. None of us know what our futures hold but we must embrace the good that is given to us, cherish it, make it a priority. I am living well with dementia; I am not letting it take away the silver linings of my life.

Monday, September 17, 2018

Yesterday I drove to Hope to meet with June Murray of Alzheimer BC, a delightful lady. We discussed the many changes that need to happen with dementia care, how the focus has to shift to the client, how organizations have to start working together and what all this might look like. However, the local chapters have no say in these matters. We did decide we wanted to grow a relationship between Alzheimer's BC and Dementia Alliance International. There is much work to be done towards this. We want to gain a good understanding of each organization and look at ways to help each other. June left me with something that I will be hanging on my wall, because I love what it implies. SUCCESS DOES NOT NECESSARILY MEAN HAPPINESS...BUT BEING HAPPY INCREASES OUR CHANCES OF FINDING SUCCESS.

Chapter Twenty-One

Saturday, December 16, 2018

Sitting here with the Christmas lights on, watching a Christmas movie, enjoying the quiet evening, drinking my 'Golden Milk,' (warm cow, almond or coconut milk, fresh ginger, coconut oil, turmeric, maybe cocoa: relaxes, aids digestion, helps fight infections and inflammation). I've been making it for four days now; sleep is improving and the brain pain has subsided again. Today I enjoyed a very peaceful day, met a couple of neighbors for a little walk through the Christmas craft sale, then it was such a beautiful warm sunny day, I took a drive to Trail, parked the car and strolled the streets checking out all the little shops, just strolling, enjoying the sights and sounds of the Christmas season, lost in my own thoughts. Does this illness scare me? Yes, it terrifies me every single day, but I rise above the fear, I choose to live as whole and complete as I can, grateful for each day even the hard ones. The hard ones make you appreciate days like today all the more.

Wednesday, February 20, 2019

I have been and still am quite ill, pneumonia, a virus infection. It's going to be a long road to regain my former wellbeing, my former strength. Stress is the biggest reason I am so sick. Prolonged stress creates serious consequences. My relationship with Jim has ended under the most sad and tragic circumstances. I won't put blame anywhere but where it belongs, on an addiction. All addictions destroy people, relationships and families. Under their influence people change; it becomes impossible for the one addicted to see the toll it takes on themselves and those around them. They believe they are in control. The truth is, without professional help, the substance controls the addict.

I truly believe my partner wanted to be able to care for me, I truly believe he loves me, I truly believe he wants the beautiful life we started to build together. I was not aware of the addiction because at the time we met he was not indulging his habit. Slowly the addiction became more powerful and, again, finally took over his whole life. With a broken heart I had to leave to save myself. Knowing an addict cannot recover if we enable them, I had to make hard decisions. The difficulties caused by the addiction created a stress overload on my system.

I came back to Vernon, to my support system which has rallied around me. It will take a long time to heal emotionally, physically and mentally. A lot of my dementia symptoms have been heightened; I am hoping that as I regain strength some of these symptoms will settle down again.

My heart breaks for a man who, beneath the addiction, is a kind, warm hearted, gentle guy; my heart breaks for losing the life that we could have had together. I wish him nothing but love and hope someday he can overcome his addiction. In the meantime, I have to make the choice to save myself.

Those closest to me said, seeing how sick this has made me, that they believe if had I stayed, my health would have spiraled down until I would not have survived. I believe they are right. I am grateful for a good doctor; I am also grateful for all those who have helped. The road to wellness begins, nutritionally, emotionally and physically, one step at a time.

Please remember to alleviate as much stress as possible from your dementia stricken loved ones. Our brains need protecting. I want people to understand the devastation addictions cause, I want people to understand the effects of addictions on others, and I want people to understand the effects of stress on those living with dementia.

My future is unknown, but I do know that being proactive and advocating will help keep me well. Those activities provide me with purpose, give me hope. I keep focused and connected and socializing. I plan to be in Los Angeles in July to speak and be part of a group of panelists. Then in November, if things stay on track, I will be speaking at a conference in Jamaica. I also want to make more of a difference at my local level, my provincial level and across Canada. I want to work on the human rights aspect of dementia. I want to ensure people are given the right to work, that they are given rehabilitation and training to ensure they continue to live as fully as possible. I want to help educate others to new possibilities.

Thursday, July 4, 2019

I'm feeling a freedom I have never experienced before; I'm less inhibited, more relaxed. I don't feel as frustrated with the difficulties my dementia creates for me, I laugh more at the blunders, I am at ease with my illness, we are one my dementia and me. Life is certainly different but it's not terrible. I focus on the good points and live for this day, this moment.

Some of the recent changes that make me less inhibited mean I don't worry about things as I once did. I was always making sure I followed all of what society said, how to dress, what's appropriate for someone my age to do and behave, I was so entrenched in all of that stuff.

Now I laugh more, I am more light-hearted, freer, I do what makes me happy. I still care for others, I still want to help others, I can just do it now with less restraints. If dementia has brought me to this place, then I'm grateful for the opportunity to truly live, to truly experience joy. I have many days and many things that are much more difficult now but I have much more enjoyment as well.

I have had opportunities I would not have, if not for my dementia: like speaking at the United Nations in New York and at a world-wide Alzheimer's Conference in Chicago. Little old me, who would have thought, I have met so many amazing people since my diagnosis. I'm happy here, right now, in this place.

Epilogue

I first met Christine the summer of 2001 when she came to Vernon to meet Uwe's mother, his brother Brent, and me. I liked her immediately; she was beautiful, funny, and full of joy.

As time progressed, she and Uwe bought a house in Valemount, and his two children, Natasha and Brenden, came to live with them permanently. Christine loved them all, volunteered for various organizations, golfed with Uwe, took the children to their sports tournaments all over the province, and created a stable home life.

In the autumn of 2003, with Uwe's full support, Christine stayed in Vernon with his mother during the week to take a two-year nursing course. She drove home after classes Friday afternoon then left early Monday morning to arrive on time for her lectures.

About 10 one night, a few months into the course, I heard a knock, opened the door and saw Christine standing there, a 'What do I do now?' look on her face and her suitcase in her hand. From then until the course was finished, she stayed at our house when school was in session. In the spring of 2005, Uwe had a tree fall on him; he too convalesced with us. Before he healed from that injury, he developed a particularly virulent form of cancer and died the 12th of June. Christine graduated that fall.

Next she obtained a job working in palliative care for Interior Health. After she sold the big house in Valemount, she bought a smaller house in Vernon thinking the children would come live with her. Instead, Natasha and Brenden decided they wanted to stay in Valemount until they graduated. She arranged for friends to board them and brought them to Vernon during school breaks until they finished school.

Later, Nicole, Christine's niece, and her two children needed a refuge; they were invited to live in her basement. For two-and-a-half years, the arrangement worked well then Nicole and her husband reconciled.

After that, when Christine's mother became bedridden; she and her husband moved in with Christine. When Christine wasn't working her regular job, she looked after her mother and those friends and family members who came to visit.

Christine sold that house and bought a condominium which would give her parents more privacy. Her mother died before they could move in. She created an upstairs suite for her stepfather then, within a year, he found a girlfriend, moved in with her and asked Chrissy for a substantial amount of money he somehow felt was owed him. Once more, she sold her home and bought a smaller place that she felt she could manage by herself.

During all this, we often discussed her inability to say no to any request on her time or resources. Slowly, she moved from thinking her worth came from being a wife, mother, daughter, or caregiver to realizing she was Christine: a loving, giving, talented, excited-about-life, independent woman with many talents.

I believe this gradual transition made it a little easier for her to come to terms with her diagnosis. She had learned to set up a few boundaries, to think of herself first on occasion, to check her schedule before undertaking new responsibilities. Acceptance of her illness did not come easy but, from the beginning, she decided she would fight for the best life possible.

Christine does not sugar-coat her experiences; her struggle is not pretty at times, but she stays positive. She has a supportive doctor, a medical background which helps her see anomalies and their possible solutions, and a few friends who stick by her through thick and thin. Others with dementia are not always so blessed.

More and more people are being diagnosed with dementia before the age of 55. They lose their livelihood, their support group, their personal possessions. They fall through the holes in the Health Care system; no one knows what to do with them. Consequently, they are starting to speak up for themselves. Christine is part of this burgeoning wave of voices shouting for the right to respectful care. These 'youngsters' may have 20 or more years of life left. They do not want to spend it just waiting to die.

Christine wants people to understand how stress and addictions impact dementia clients and, indirectly, their caregivers and friends. She cannot bring herself to write details about her relationship with Jim but gave me permission to voice my observations.

Christine's friendship with Jim, beginning in June, 2018, brought a great deal of joy into her life. Those of us who met him knew him as a kind, gentle man with a good sense of humor. He did have health issues and suffered a small stroke soon after they met. He often forgot to take his medicines.

As their friendship blossomed, Christine helped him remember to take his pills, his physical health improved and work became a possibility. They met in

164

person the long weekend in August and felt like old friends meeting after a long absence.

Their relationship may have progressed at a slower rate under normal conditions, but Christine's landlord decided to sell her apartment and Jim landed a job in Kamloops requiring him to move south. At the end of August, they agreed to combine households and live in Jim's trailer wherever his work took him. For the first while they lived in Spences Bridge and were very happy. Phoebe sometimes neglected Christine to follow Jim around or sit on his lap.

In mid-September, Christine stayed at Ross and Brenda's place. She watched their sick dog while they worked nights and she worked a few days for the car dealership in Vernon. At that time her relationship with Jim was going well and she was beaming. By September 26th they were officially engaged.

On October 3rd, I met Jim for the first time and liked him immediately. He was shy at first, but by the end of the evening he was laughing and joking. The rest of Chrissy's friends liked him as well. We were ready to accept him wholeheartedly.

Christine and Jim came to visit in mid-October, the day before they moved the trailer to Castlegar, his new place of employment. She told me he had started drinking one or two drinks after supper most evenings.

One Thursday afternoon, November 1st, they came again to stay over. Jim was looking healthier than ever and Christine was radiant. After seeing doctors and visiting with Ross and Brenda, Christine did mention that if Jim had more than two drinks, he became insulting. They left Saturday morning.

Again, on a Thursday, November 15th, Christine and Jim came for the weekend and stayed at Ross and Brenda's. Christine planned a birthday party for Jim at a restaurant here in town, complete with a birthday cake. She invited Brent and me, Ross and Brenda, Ivor and Barb, Cindy and Les. Brent was out of town working so Christine invited Les' brother, who was unexpectedly visiting, to join us. Both Brenda and I noticed that partway through the dinner, Jim made a decision that pleased him. I thought he had decided he could be himself with us, Brenda, in retrospect, thought he decided he had us fooled. I think we may have both been right. I know he ordered a third drink.

Christine seemed wary and watchful the next day. I suggested she should relax but she told me Jim had said many hurtful things the night before, calling her horrible names and telling her all his problems were her fault. Red flags went up all over.

Things deteriorated from there. Christine found empty rum bottles hidden in the luggage they had used coming to Vernon. His liquor consumption went up weekly. Jim's family hadn't told Christine that their dad was an alcoholic because his health issues had kept him sober for several months and they hoped that finding a good woman would give him incentive to stay that way.

Phoebe started avoiding Jim, hiding in another room when he wanted to pet her. Christine couldn't keep up her walking or Keto diet, didn't get the sleep she needed, was away from her physiotherapist's steady treatments, was stressed all the time. Finally, she started taking one-day road trips to various towns, plus visiting friends and family to get away from the situation in the trailer.

Sunday, January 20th, 2019, Christine moved into our basement suite to house sit for three weeks. By the time we came back she had her own apartment and was recovering from pneumonia and a serious lack of oxygen intake. Much of the hard work she had put into stabilizing her health had been undone. She and a friend with a large SUV went back to Jim's trailer to pick up the rest of her belongings and to take back some items he had in her storage unit.

Here is a quote from Christine's journal entry of March 6, 2017. "I was visiting with one of my lovely friends yesterday and we were discussing taking opportunities when they come along. She understands how short life truly is and she said something that I feel is so true and so much of what I try to express but can't so I will quote her. 'I would rather live with the regret of taking an opportunity that failed to work out, than to live with the regret of not taking the opportunity at all.'"

This is how Christine feels about her relationship with Jim.

Christine is slowly healing. Her new apartment is even nicer than the one she gave up and is as well situated. Friends and family helped her replace household items she had disposed of. The plant nursery who hired her in 2017 asked her to work four hours on Saturday and Sunday as her health allows. She is doing odd jobs for friends, is busy with DAI board business, has just filmed a part in a documentary on people with dementia, and is planning on speaking at a United Nations Conference held in New York in June. The woman never quits.

END

Denise bought for me! aug 13/2020